TOTAL QUALITY
Key Terms and Concepts

William L. Duncan
Luftig & Warren International

American Management Association

New York • Atlanta • Boston • Chicago • Kansas City • San Francisco • Washington, D. C.
Brussels • Mexico City • Tokyo • Toronto

Library of Congress Cataloging-in-Publication Data

Duncan, William L.
    Total quality : key terms and concepts / [William L. Duncan].
        p.   cm.
    Includes bibliographical references.
    ISBN 0-8144-7876-X
    1. Total quality management—Dictionaries.   I. Title.
    HD62.15.D86   1995
    658.5'62'03—dc20

                                                                95-33989
                                                                CIP

Printing number

10   9   8   7   6   5   4   3   2   1

Introduction

Total quality management (TQM) implementation is a lifelong, company-wide commitment. It involves broad, sweeping change across the organization and deep, fundamental process improvement. In most organizations, the very culture of the company is restructured.

This book is a desk reference for TQM practitioners who have undertaken the TQM journey and for anyone interested in quality improvement, a core element for organizational success. The definitions and discussions of key quality terms and concepts help provide a better understanding of the various aspects of the quality field. To help facilitate this learning process, boldface type is used to highlight terms or phrases that are defined within the glossary portion of this book. Because of the fundamental, culture-based nature of TQM-related change, it is important to provide the following elements in a reference book like this one:

1. *A general framework for ready reference that outlines the phases of TQM implementation.* An overview of the phases of successful TQM implementation is provided in this Introduction, and each phase is detailed in individual listings within the publication's definitions. The outline should allow practitioners to quickly reference this book for (1) an objective benchmark of the types of activities that should be completed or under way at any point in the TQM implementation process and (2) a general understanding of what lies ahead. This information will also prove invaluable in developing introductory and overview materials about how TQM implementations work and what they involve. (A detailed implementation plan is not included here, since many already exist in popular TQM books, and the specifics of each implementation plan vary greatly from organization to organization, reflecting the needs of the company involved.)

2. *A glossary of TQM terminology.* Cultures are held together not only by a system of values and beliefs, but also by a common language. The language of TQM is unique, and most of the terminology involved is listed and defined within this text. Related terms are cross-references as appropriate. Glossary entries span the entire spectrum of the quality field—from technical terms such as *Poisson distribution* to less technical but more frequently used terms such as *empowerment*. (Note that a term may be more commonly used without necessarily being more commonly understood!)

The Phases of TQM Implementation—An Overview

Phase I: Preparation Phase

Phase I involves an examination of the business—its objectives, problems, and customer needs. During this phase, management decides whether to use TQM or another approach to meet the needs of all of the company's stakeholders. For more detailed information, see the entry **preparation phase (phase I)** in the glossary portion of this text.

Phase II: Planning Phase

The second phase consists of the following steps: (1) securing of commitments; (2) establishment of the business lead team, company steering committee, and process improvement team structures; (3) strategic planning and policy deployment; (4) development of the implementation plan; and (5) awareness training. For more detailed information, see the entry **planning phase (phase II)** in the glossary portion of this text.

Phase III: Assessment Phase

This phase consists of identifying the structure, strengths, and weaknesses of the organization, competition, products and services, work force, and customers. At the conclusion of this phase, there should be a clear understanding of customer needs, how well the organization fulfills those needs, and where the organization's processes need to be strengthened to improve customer satisfaction and gain market share. For more detailed information, see the entry **assessment phase (phase III)** in the glossary portion of this text.

Phase IV: Implementation Phase

Also called the *deployment phase*, this phase of TQM implementation includes the following steps: (1) alignment of the program with strategic plans, (2) strengthening the program infrastructure, (3) initiating continuous improvement activities, (4) monitoring performance, and (5) communicating lessons learned. At the conclusion of this phase, there should be a strong, ongoing TQM-based continuous improvement process in place with tangible benefits manifested. For more detailed information, see the entry **implementation phase (phase IV)** in the glossary portion of this text.

Phase V: Networking Phase

In the final phase of TQM implementation, initial TQM successes are exploited, leveraging them to stimulate broader improvements throughout the organization, and reaching out into the supplier community. The organization (1) communicates strategic improvement plans with outside organizations, (2) shares lessons learned with these key organizations, (3) initiates regular visits with suppliers and customers to cement the bonds of understanding and mutual growth, (4) institutionalizes the improvement process throughout the customer/producer/supplier chain, and (5) develops the process into a continuous "loop" that assures sustainability. For more detailed information, see the entry **networking phase (phase V)** in the glossary portion of this text.

A

ABC   See **activity-based costing.**

absolutes of quality management   A set of principles that include:

1. **Quality** means **conformance**, not elegance.
2. There is no such thing as a quality problem.
3. There is no such thing as the economics of quality; it is always cheaper to do the job right the first time.
4. The only performance measurement is the **cost of quality**.
5. The only performance standard is **zero defects**.

acceptable quality level (AQL)   The percentage of **defects** that are acceptable without rejecting an entire **lot** sampled. This concept, developed in the 1940s, contradicts the philosophy of **TQM** in many important ways: It allows defects to pass through to the final product, it implicitly encourages **suppliers** to ship **defective** materials to their **customers**, and it reduces **quality** to a statistical game in which the customer is the ultimate loser. Also called **acceptance number.**

acceptance number   See **acceptable quality level.**

accountability   The level of **ownership** perceived by **TQM** participants and shown in their actions. Accountability requires defined responsibility, acceptance/**ownership** of that responsibility, understanding of the **objective** and how one's actions influence achievement of that objective, and some level of enthusiasm for attaining the stated objective. Enthusiasm may result from positive incentives (e.g., financial rewards). See also **reward and recognition system.**

accreditation   The credential-establishing action of official registrars. In relation to achieving **International Standards Organization** registration, the **ISO** dictionary defines *accreditation* as "a favorable assessment by the **Registrar Accreditation Board** in the United States or a counterpart in another nation attesting to a registrar's requirements with applicable requirements."

accuracy   The degree to which a **measurement process** conforms to a predetermined standard or accepted reference value. It is important to distinguish between accuracy and **precision**; they are not synonymous. Being precise might imply that the variation from measure to measure on the same specimen is extremely small, or for that matter, practically nonexistent. However, unless the measured value for the **characteristic** falls at or near the **true value** of the master specimen or standard, the sample measures will all be precisely wrong. The degree to which the mean of repeated measures of a given specimen or standard varies from the true value is a measure of the **bias** of the measurement process. Unbiased measurement processes are said to be accurate; biased processes are said to be in need of **calibration**. See also **conformance**.

activity-based costing (ABC)   A cost accounting process that begins with the premise that products consume activities and that the activities in turn consume resources (rather than beginning with the premise that products consume resources). ABC differs significantly from traditional methods of accounting and is much more supportive of **TQM**-related improvement activities. By identifying the **cost driver** activities, a much more accurate picture of costs associated with any given product can be obtained. The two major elements of ABC systems are the **process value analysis** and the cost driver analysis. The culmination of these efforts provides tight linkage between financial performance and quality improvement activities.

adding value   Taking action that enhances the satisfaction of **customer needs**, and does so at a minimum cost in a safe environment. The customer may be a downstream internal customer or an end consumer of the product. See also **customer, internal** and **customer satisfaction**.

advanced procurement technology (APT)   A field of **just-in-time manufacturing** that integrates a **supplier's** operations as closely as possible with those of its **customer**. In essence, partnerships are formed between suppliers and customers. Specific elements of APT include (1) data sharing, (2) improved ordering devices and methods, (3) **commodity-based contract-**

ing, (4) comprehensive supplier performance measures, (5) supplier certi-fication, (6) effective buyer evaluation criteria, (7) joint supplier-customer cost reduction initiatives, (8) supplier **JIT training**, and (9) enhancements in the procurement organization structure.

1. *Data sharing* means the sharing of data between a manufac-turer and a supplier to improve response time, increase **efficiency**, and foster trust between the two organizations. Sharing data in this fashion, especially with the manufacturer's most important suppliers, can provide vital early warning signs of impending changes in vol-umes, delivery dates, and capacity constraints that could have sub-stantive impact on the ability to deliver purchased parts on time. However, effective data sharing can usually only be accomplished when the supplier base has been narrowed to avoid risks associated with industrial espionage and general leaking of competition-sensi-tive data. Among the specific types of data that are commonly shared with suppliers in advanced **TQM** environments are production schedules, sales forecasts, design data, packaging requirements, **dis-tribution** methods and volumes, and field service reports pertaining to the supplier-provided components and materials.

2. *Improved ordering devices and methods* typically include **elec-tronic data interchange** equipment (hardware and software) and "pull"-type ordering methods similar to the Japanese **kanban** tech-niques. (See **pull system**.) **EDI** can make the sharing of data, place-ment of orders, revision of designs, and other important data ex-changes virtually instantaneous. The pulling of material via a kanban approach turns a part of the suppliers' manufacturing capacity into an extension of their customers' operations. It is a remarkably effec-tive means to eliminate **work-in-process** queues of parts and mate-rial.

3. *Commodity-based contracting* is a purchase agreement written to cover an entire **commodity** of parts or materials. Combining the requirements for all the parts within a commodity frequently pro-vides enough volume-based leverage to create efficiency and flexibil-ity advantages for both suppliers and their customers.

4. *Comprehensive supplier performance measures* are metrics used to track a supplier's performance, such as price, delivery, product **qual-ity**, financial stability, geographic proximity, special advantages (such as providing an opportunity to enter foreign markets), capacity for

growth, and the willingness to share data, undertake consignment arrangements, and do commodity-based contracting, specialized containering, and **JIT** and pull-based manufacturing.

5. *Supplier certification* is a state achieved when the buyer gains an adequate level of confidence in the suppliers' process **controls** in order to eliminate the need for incoming **inspection** activity. At this point, infrequent **random sample** spot checks and the process control data of suppliers' **processes** are adequate to ensure supplier product quality.

6. *Effective buyer evaluation criteria* in a **TQM** environment include quality and delivery performance of the buyer's supplier base, cost containment and reduction, supplier **lead time** reduction, percent of time spent at supplier facilities, and effectiveness in joint cost reduction/profitability efforts with suppliers. Additional criteria being used include ongoing education efforts and material inventory turn rates.

7. *Joint supplier-customer cost-reduction initiatives* involve the collaboration of professionals from multiple disciplines (typically including engineering, production, and quality assurance) from both the customer and supplier organizations with the purpose of reducing the cost of the purchased goods. Any success in this area is then shared equally between the supplier and the customer.

8. *Supplier JIT training* involves developing a **training** team from the customer facility and/or from an outside consulting agency to train a supplier in the application of **TQM** (and specifically **JIT**) principles in its operations. See also **education and training (for total quality)**.

9. *Enhancements in the procurement organization structure* may include the adoption of buyer-planner job responsibilities (combined responsibilities of the former requirements planner and buyer functions) and the organization of procurement professionals' responsibilities around commodities.

advanced quality planning (AQP) The process of designing final **quality** into the product at the planning and engineering stage rather than after manufacturing has been initiated. This concept is essential in developing **robust** product designs and is fundamental to **concurrent engineering**.

affinity diagram   A tool that assists in problem definition/resolution by organizing ideas according to recognized relationships (levels of affinity) between them. In **TQM** activities, the technique is most often applied as a form of **brainstorming** where ideas about potential causes of problems and symptoms are put on Post-it notes as quickly as they can be identified by a group, then more deliberately organized into clusters that appear by group **consensus** to be related to each other. This tool is frequently used together with a **relationship diagram** to map various symptoms to causal factors in **problem solving strategy** (see Figure 1).

AI   See **artificial intelligence**.

alpha (α)   The probability of making a **Type I error**; that is, rejecting a **hypothesis** when it is true. For **control charts**, the probability that we think a **process** is out of control although it is still in **control**.

Figure 1. Affinity diagram for problem-solving tools.

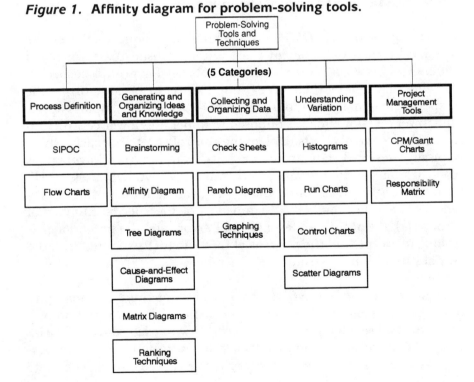

American National Standards Institute (ANSI) An organization founded in 1918 for the purpose of eliminating redundancies and conflicts among the standards developed within industry. ANSI is the U.S. member of the **International Standards Organization**, which is based in Geneva, Switzerland. The **ISO** is, in turn, the originating body for **ISO 9000** quality standards.

American Productivity and Quality Center (APQC) An organization based in Houston, Texas, that does extensive work in **quality** and **TQM** consulting and has an especially strong practice in the area of **benchmarking**. The APQC was founded in 1977 and currently has approximately 300 members.

American Society for Quality Control (ASQC) A professional organization for **quality assurance** and quality management professionals. Based in Milwaukee, Wisconsin, this organization was founded in 1946 and today has more than 120,000 members.

AMH See **automated material handling**.

analysis of means (ANOM) An analytical technique that uses the graphical format of a **control chart** in the (statistical) assessment of differences between group summary statistics for groups suspected of being different by their preexisting nature, or because of specific (experimental) manipulations. The ANOM technique employs upper and lower decision limits as opposed to upper and lower control limits used on control charts. Unlike the control chart approach, which typically uses $\pm$ 3 standard error units around a grand average as control limits for the relevant group statistics, the ANOM uses $\pm$ "H" standard error units around the grand average for assessing differences. The value for "H" is a function of the specific number of groups *(k)*, the **alpha** risk level (**Type I error** rate) the practitioner is willing to accept, and the **degrees of freedom (df)** associated with the **variability** within the groups being studied.

analysis of variance (ANOVA) A statistical method for analyzing data, usually resulting from an experiment. The total variation of a data set is subdivided into parts associated with each source of variation so that **variance** components can be estimated, or a **hypothesis(es)** can be tested related to the **parameters** of the model. The three basic calculational models are fixed, random, and mixed, often referred to as Model I, Model II, and Model III respectively.

ANOM   See **analysis of means**.

ANOVA   See **analysis of variance**.

ANSI   See **American National Standards Institute**.

AOQ   See **average outgoing quality**.

APP   See **automated process planning**.

appraisal costs   The costs resulting from formal evaluations of **quality** levels and for maintaining the documentation associated with **conformance** to company quality standards. These costs include labor (typically **inspection** time), measurement equipment (from scales and micrometers to x-ray equipment), and associated costs such as source inspectors' travel expenses. Part of a **cost of quality** accounting system.

APQC   See **American Productivity and Quality Center**.

APT   See **advanced procurement technology**.

AQL   See **acceptable quality level**.

AQP   See **advanced quality planning**.

architecture, business   See **business architecture**.

architecture, information systems   The fundamental design of the information system. This design dictates the standards for all devices, software, and user interfaces. It defines the capability and capacity of the systems and is the principal guideline for all subsequent systems development.
    The information systems architecture is at the core of progressive manufacturing and service companies and will prove to be critical to providing the kind of responsiveness and process **control** required for success in the decades ahead. Industry will move toward

seamless systems consisting of integrated workstations, database management systems, servers, and some application-specific systems for departmental use.

Typical information systems and communication systems architectures are depicted in Figures 2a and 2b.

arithmetic mean   For any set of values, the average or the sum of the values divided by the number of values summed. It is typically denoted in **quality** applications by $\bar{X}$ or X-bar. See also **mean**.

Figure 2a. **Typical integrated information systems architecture (1995–2005).**

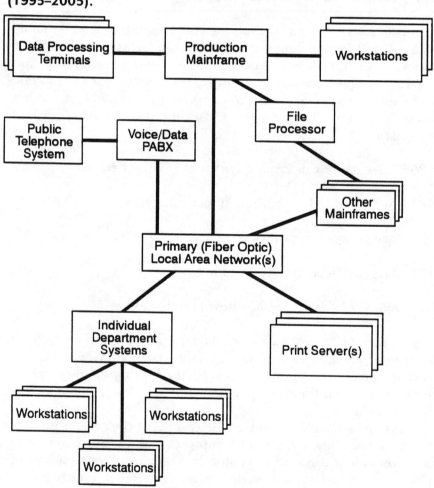

Figure 2b. Typical communication systems architecture (1995–2005).

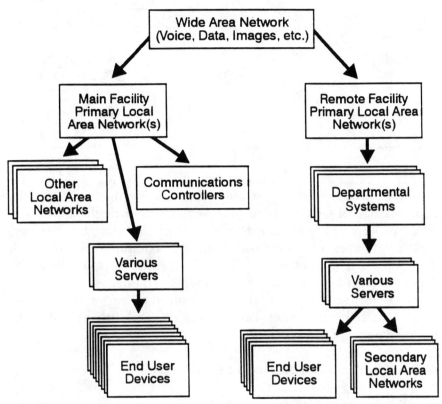

arrow diagram   A popular term describing the output of the PERT process and often called a **PERT chart**. A chart defining the precedence and time spans of the sequence of events required to produce a desired outcome. Often used as the top-level tool for monitoring large projects with many interrelated steps because of its ability to succinctly demonstrate complex relationships and interdependencies (see Figure 3). See also **program evaluation and review technique**.

artificial intelligence (AI)   A branch of computer science that deals with the development of computers that can "think." The two primary thrusts of AI explored most extensively to date are expert systems and natural language processors. Expert systems are especially relevant in the **quality** field because they enable us to capture some level of human expertise in decision tree form within a computer.

Figure 3. **Arrow diagram/PERT chart.**

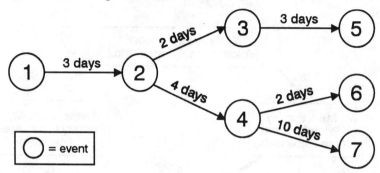

This results in a **decision support system** that provides guidance for people in **problem solving strategy**, by allowing them to apply the expertise of more experienced professionals in the field. Natural language processors are of value to the quality field as well because they make it far easier for people with little or no computer experience or **training** to use the machines effectively. Basically, natural language processing technology teaches computers to communicate in human language (through voice synthesizers, optical character recognition, etc.) so that the computer can listen, talk, and correspond using human language.

ASQC   See **American Society for Quality Control**.

assemble-to-forecast   A production approach in which assembly orders are launched based on forecasted sales, typically offset by a standard assembly time.

assemble-to-order   A production approach in which products are only assembled when an actual sales order is received. Final assembly of the end product is never based on a forecast or as the result of a desire for work load stability. This approach is in direct contrast to the **assemble-to-stock** or **assemble-to-forecast** approaches.

assemble-to-stock   A production approach in which final assembly is initiated based on the need to maintain a minimum level of finished goods (or *stock*) in inventory. As finished stock is depleted beyond a designated reorder point, an assembly order for additional products is launched.

assembly, design for   See **design for assembly**.

assessment phase (phase III)   The third major phase of a **TQM** implementation plan. (See the Introduction for an overview of all five phases.) This phase involves identifying the structure, strengths, and weaknesses of:

- Internal organization and processes
- Competition
- External products and services
- Customer
- Work force skill levels

It is the primary information-gathering phase of the TQM plan, resulting in an in-depth understanding of the organization's current state and potential opportunities. Many companies use the **Malcolm Baldrige National Quality Award** criteria as a guide for their internal assessment activities, and others use one or more of the **ISO 9000** quality standards as a road map. While it overlaps most of the other phases of the TQM implementation, the assessment phase typically begins in about the second month and runs for about two years. (Note that it is not necessary to wait until the end of the assessment phase before you can expect positive results from a TQM implementation. Because of the overlapping activities with other phases, positive results often begin to materialize after about eighteen months.)

The **objective** of the assessment phase is to achieve a clear understanding of the organization, the products and services of the organization, the customers, and the competitors. The assessment phase is the first phase of a TQM program that really gets a significant part of the organization involved and attempts to garner support and commitment from the employee base.

The assessment phase begins with a review of the company's **vision** and/or **mission statement(s)**. As the mission is driven down through the organization, all employees must understand how their individual roles tie into that mission, who their **customers** are, and how their customers judge whether they are receiving good **value**.

The internal organization should be thoroughly assessed to understand its own **company culture**, **processes**, products and services, and internal supplier/customer relationships. A **gap analysis** should then be performed, based on the company's mission and the current culture, to identify the desired **characteristics** of the future company culture; the technologies, skills, and process characteristics desired in the future state; and what work will be required to achieve that future culture. Many analytical tools described throughout this text come into play in the assessment phase, including **Pareto charts**, **brainstorming**, and **cause-and-effect** analysis.

Developing an understanding of the products and services of the organization requires the identification of the company's **critical process characteristics** that result in the **quality**, **reliability**, price, and maintainability of the products or services provided. This is often accomplished through both traditional and innovative applications of **quality function deployment**.

Developing an understanding of the customers' expectations (see **expectations, customer**) and level of satisfaction (see **customer satisfaction**) involves the application of several tools and techniques, including regular formal customer surveys, customer involvement in design processes, QFD applications to external customers' stated desires, and special **teams** of important current and potential customers drawn into regular design and product assessment activities.

To understand the competitor base, an organization needs to **benchmark** its products and processes against those considered "best in class" by the organization's customers.

asset utilization   The product of the **availability**, **duty cycle**, **efficiency**, and **recovery** of an operation.

assignable causes   See **special causes**.

attribute data   Discrete data (**nominal data** and **ordinal data**). Typical attribute **control charts** are **p-charts** (proportion **defective**), **np-charts** (number defective), **c-charts** (number of **defects**), and **u-charts** (average number of defects per unit).

attributes tracking   A summary of **go/no go** conditions, such as within/not within **tolerance**. Uses the **c-chart** and **np-chart** if measuring a **sample** whose size remains constant, or **p-charts** and **u-charts** where the sample size varies.

audit   The formal and systematic **inspection** or review of **processes** to ensure compliance to predefined requirements, or the action of performing such an inspection.

automated material handling (AMH) The handling of material (packaging, movement, storage, or retrieval) by automated systems and devices. This aspect of materials management is becoming increasingly popular in quality improvement programs for eliminating data entry errors through automated identification of material (**bar coding**, optical character recognition, etc.) and the automated tracking of storage and retrieval transactions.

automated process planning (APP) The automatic generation of production process routings and high-level work instructions from **computer-aided process planning** systems.

automation The performance of work by machines. This process involves designing both the work tasks and the equipment involved to support automated operations, including designed-in **process capability** and **reliability**. These attributes of automation are demonstrated by the consistency of the **process** in producing goods that conform to all **specifications**. See also **conformance**.

availability The (total time) minus (scheduled, unscheduled, and idle downtime) divided by (the total time for the operation).

average (X-bar) See **arithmetic mean**.

average and range chart (X-bar and R chart) A variables **control chart** that depicts sample **means** (averages) and ranges for assessing and maintaining statistical control of **continuous data** processes. The **range chart** is used to assess the **variability** associated with the **population**. The mean ($\overline{X}$ or X-bar) is employed to assess the **central tendency** of the **process**. If the process is in a state of statistical control, data from the two charts together may be used to assess the capability of the process.

average (mean) chart A **control chart** that uses the **sample** or **subgroup** average, X-bar, to determine the **stability** of the process **mean**.

average outgoing quality (AOQ) The expected level of **quality** in products from a designated **process**. (This concept implicitly states that some level of quality less than 100% is expected.)

B

backflushing   A systematic approach to inventory accounting that relieves quantities from inventory based on the assumption that when the next assembly is used (or consumed), the components required to build it have also necessarily been consumed. Therefore, when a product is sold from the last assembly operation, all of the parts that go into that assembly may be automatically removed from inventory by the material accounting system. Some companies involved in **just-in-time manufacturing** operations use this method to trigger payment to their suppliers.

Baldrige Award   See **Malcolm Baldrige National Quality Award**.

Band-Aid approach   A popular expression used to describe responses to problems involving temporary solutions (that usually address symptoms) rather than permanent fixes (that address the **root cause**). Examples include increasing fabrication order quantities to overcome high scrap levels in production, and adding **lead time** to the ordering cycle for purchased parts in response to part shortages.

barbell chart   See **histogram**.

bar coding   A means of identification that uses information encoded in a series of vertical bars printed close to one another on the surface of an object. Data from the bar code are interpreted by an electronic scan, usually attached to a computer system. This is an extremely popular means of part, product, and package identification in many industries, and manufacturing companies are finding widespread usages, primarily in inventory **control** and labor accounting areas.

basic tools of experimental design   A group of methods commonly associated with the conduct of experiments based on modern methods, generally including **planned grouping**, **randomization**, and **replication**. See also **experimental design** and **design of experiments.**

batch manufacturing　An approach to **lot** sizing for production operations that produces parts in large groups to maximize the production yielded from a single occurrence of setup cost. Batch size (or **lot size**) is typically decided in these environments using a formula called *economic order quantity* (EOQ). EOQ divides the holding cost of inventory by the setup cost associated with multiple production runs and establishes an optimum lot size.

batch size　See **lot size**.

bathtub curve　See **reliability modeling**.

bell-shaped curve/distribution　A graphic display of measurement occurrences that, when plotted, gives the appearance of a bell shape because the occurrences stack up on each side of a central point, tapering off in frequency as the occurrences are farther removed from the center. The **normal distribution** is an example of a bell-shaped curve.

benchmarking　A technique used to identify performance levels in predefined areas from company to company, or, less often, between sister factories within the same company. The technique provides an opportunity for companies to compare their own performance in certain areas against other companies considered the best at the operation being examined. When benchmarked companies compete for the same markets, the process is known as competitive benchmarking. (See also **competitor influences**.) Benchmarking has a track record of demonstrated success, particularly among some American companies (such as the Xerox Corporation) regarded within their industries as **quality** leaders. The benchmarking process compares methods and results of **processes** and practices and may be applied in both manufacturing and service environments.

　　Often, companies looking for others considered "best in class" against whom to benchmark begin with a list of recent winners of the **Malcolm Baldrige National Quality Award**. Some companies use the base of **ISO 9000** registered companies as a starting point. Other potential sources include the *Thomas Register*, trade journals, and trade shows.

　　The ten-step benchmarking approach most commonly cited grew out of the Xerox activity in this area during the 1980s. The steps are:

　　1. Identify those processes or practices to be benchmarked, typically based on relevance to **customer satisfaction**.

2. Identify the base of companies against whom a comparison will be made.
3. Identify **data collection** methods and collect the data.
4. Identify current performance levels (clear both internal and at compared-to companies) and note differences. For every significant gap in performance (positive or negative), identify the causes.
5. Establish targets for future performance levels. They should be based on not only existing performance levels at compared-to companies, but also the targets that companies have set for their own future performance.
6. Communicate findings to management, process owners, and **stakeholders** to garner acceptance of reality and enthusiasm for improvement.
7. Establish intermediate functional **goals** that will support the achievement of targets established in step 5. Solicit stakeholder and process owner participation in improvement strategies as they are developed.
8. Develop detailed implementation plans and assign responsibilities for each significant action.
9. Implement improvement activity. Monitor progress and take **corrective action** as required to maintain momentum.
10. Recalibrate benchmarks and begin the process all over again. Make benchmarking an aspect of **continuous improvement**.

best practice   See **operator-controllable error**.

beta (β)   In **statistical quality control** the probability of making a **Type II error**; that is, of accepting a **hypothesis** as true when it is false. For **control charts**, the probability that we think the **process** is still in **control** even though it is out of control.

bias   A systematic error that contributes to the difference between an accepted reference value and an observed **sample** mean.

big Q, little q   An expression used to indicate the difference between managing for a comprehensive **quality** approach in all aspects of business (big Q) and managing for quality in a limited area, such as factory **processes** or products (little q).

bimodal distribution   See **double-peaked distribution**.

binomial distribution   The **distribution** of probability that a specified number of successes will occur within a given number of independent trials (assuming that the probability of success in each trial is the same). This distribution relates to discrete random variables (**nominal data**). It takes the form

$$\left[\frac{n!}{r!\,(n-r)!}\right]p^r q^{n-r}$$

See Figure 4.

blanket orders   A purchase order for a part or a part family that contains part numbers, part descriptions, and prices (when possible), but no specific order quantities. Blanket orders typically indicate only an estimated usage over the period of time covered by the contract. Actual shipments are authorized by the buyer as the parts are

Figure 4. **Binomial distribution.**

Calculation of Probabilities for Binomial Distributions

Probability of Occurrence (p):   0.8 $np = 6,400$

Number of Trials (n):   8

Number of Occurrences (r):   0

r	Prob at r	Equal & Above	Equal & Below
0	0.000	1.000	0.000
1	0.000	1.000	0.000
2	0.001	1.000	0.001
3	0.009	0.999	0.010
4	0.046	0.990	0.056
5	0.147	0.944	0.203
6	0.294	0.797	0.497
7	0.336	0.503	0.832
8	0.168	0.168	1.000

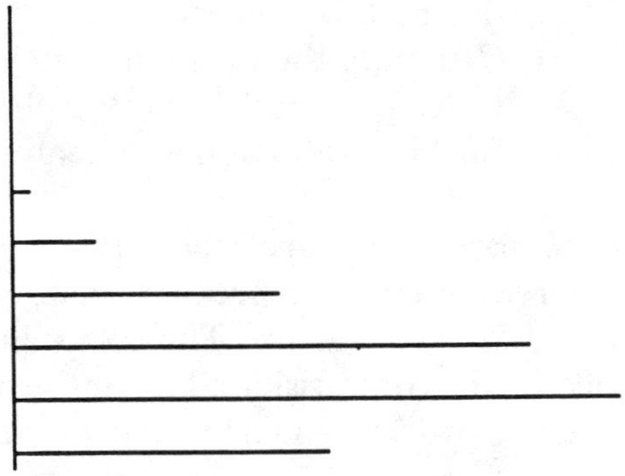

needed. At the end of the period covered, the order may or may not be renewed at the discretion of either party. This type of order is frequently used in **just-in-time manufacturing** environments where operations can be streamlined and individual releases may be made via telephone authorization or an **electronic data interchange** link.

block diagram   A diagram made up of simple blocks (squares and rectangles) depicting the operations and interrelationships within a specified system. The blocks represent the system elements (major activities or **processes**), and the arrows between them represent flows of data or materials. Block diagrams are an excellent way to quickly and effectively communicate the basic operations of a system. See also **flow chart**.

blueprint diagram/tolerance   See **specification limits**.

boundaries   In a frequency **histogram**, lines that distinguish between each interval shown in a sequence. In operations documentation, vertical lines that distinguish between the end of one **process** and the beginning of the next process or horizontal lines that distinguish management **spans of control**.

brainstorming   Usually a **team**-based activity used to develop group **consensus** on probable causes for a specified problem. The **objective** is to capture as many ideas as possible. The technique involves:

1. Defining the problem clearly for the group.
2. Soliciting and recording ideas from the group about potential causes. (Typically, a **facilitator** records the suggestions as quickly as the group can call them out. No criticism is allowed during this process.)
3. Grouping the causes into similar categories, throwing out the ridiculous, and retaining the grouped plausible causes for further evaluation and analysis.

breakthrough improvements   Dramatic positive changes in product or service **quality** or **process** (manufacturing, assembly, administrative, etc.) performance. These changes are typically accomplished by specifically commissioned teams using one of several disciplined strategies working on a regular *released time* basis to accomplish a specific mission or **objective**. Breakthrough improvements are large, step-function improvements as contrasted with incremental small **continuous improvements** described and characterized by **kaizen**.

buffer inventory/stock Inventory ordered or manufactured and stored in excess of real demands to compensate for uncertainty in downstream manufacturing or sales. Buffer inventory may be accumulated at various stages, such as at the point between subassembly and final assembly, to soften the peaks and valleys of production demand and maintain more direct labor work load **stability**. Buffer inventory (or buffer stock) is generally regarded by supporters of TQM, and especially by advocates of **just-in-time manufacturing**, to be an example of **waste** that should be targeted for elimination.

business architecture The operating and organizational structure of a business, including all major **processes** and systems.

business architecture model A model developed by Svenson, Wallace, Wallace, and Wexler in *The Quality Roadmap* (New York: AMACOM, 1993) that depicts business as a cube. On the face of the cube there are three horizontal layers consisting of **business drivers**, **business processes** and metrics, and **resource infrastructure**. On the side of the cube are four vertical slices containing assess, design, deploy, and integrate elements. On the underside of the cube are three additional front-to-back vertical slices comprised of executive, middle management, and working level. The developers believe that this model of business offers an effective alternative to functional silo perspectives on business operation.

business drivers Factors vital to the business performance of a company and its ability to compete in the marketplace. Examples include assets, competencies, marketplace factors, and **stakeholder** requirements. Business drivers are best defined by the **customer** and are extremely useful in identifying perceived strengths and weaknesses for strategic planning and candidates for TQM improvement initiatives.

business lead team See discussion under **planning phase (phase II)**.

business plan A company's operating plan and a fundamental element of **policy deployment**. It should contain a restatement of the company's **mission statement**, long-term milestones, and the metrics associated with each milestone. These data should include progress-to-date, remaining gaps, and strategies to be used in attaining the milestones listed.

The business plan is generally developed and deployed annually. Once the long-range strategic plan is developed, the business plan becomes the primary vehicle for evaluating and documenting progress toward long-range milestones.

business processes   Functional activities within an organization that typically fall into the following three categories:

1. *Group of **processes** that are found along the value chain*. In a manufacturing company, **value-adding processes** include product/process definition, production, **distribution**, and product/customer support. This is the most important category. See **value**.
2. *Support processes*. Procurement, industrial engineering, tooling production, machine maintenance, and receiving and shipping are processes that are required to directly support the value-added processes.
3. *Processes that bear little direct relationship to the value-added processes, but are still a necessary part of any business* (e.g., most accounting and finance processes, business development processes, and strategic planning).

It is important to note that most processes cross the boundary lines of multiple functional organizations within a company, especially in those companies with traditional functional organization structures. Increasingly, businesses recognize the need to manage by process rather than by function, and this recognition is giving rise to more horizontal **spans of control** and far greater effectiveness in management.

C

c-chart   A type of **control chart**, based on the normal approximation of the **Poisson distribution**, that shows the number of **defects** for sample **subgroups** that are of equal size (see Figure 5).

CAD   See **computer-aided design**.

calibration   The comparison of a measurement instrument or system with unknown or questionable **accuracy** to one for which the accuracy is known. This process is performed to determine the accuracy of the first system, identifying the type and degree of any variation from the required performance specification. In a limited sense, calibration is also used to describe the elimination of **bias** from a measurement process by moving the mean of the **measurement error** distribution to the **true value** of a standard or master specimen.

capability, process   See **process capability**.

CAPP   See **computer-aided process planning**.

cause and effect   A popular expression used to describe the relationship between a condition or event and the results from that condition or event. There may be both direct and indirect results from any given cause. A combination of factors may be required for a causal situation to occur, and multiple effects may result from a given cause or set of causes.

cause-and-effect diagram   A tool used to identify relationships between specific effects and their **root causes**. This tool is often called the **Ishikawa diagram**, the fishbone diagram, and the Ishikawa fishbone diagram. Originally developed by Kaoru Ishikawa, the diagram has the structure of a fish skeleton when it has been completed. Properly used, the diagram helps to determine the main causes and subcauses that have resulted in

Figure 5. c-chart.

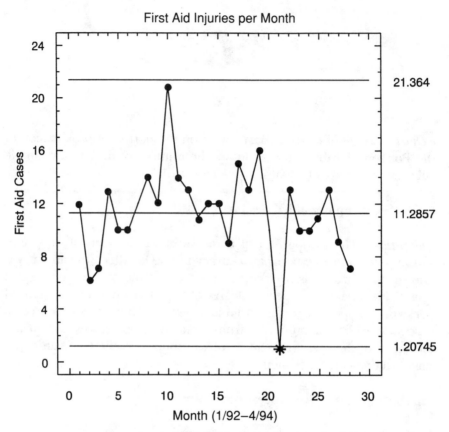

NOTE: The point below the lower limit of expected variation (21st month) indicates that there was something different about that month that led to fewer injuries (e.g., equipment down).

an effect (symptom) or **quality** problem (see Figure 6). See also **dispersion analysis**.

cause, common See **common causes**.

cause, root See **root cause**.

CDE See **compound document exchange**.

cellular manufacturing A production approach that uses groupings of manufacturing equipment, tools, and people organized to perform an en-

Figure 6. Cause-and-effect diagram: maintenance costs.

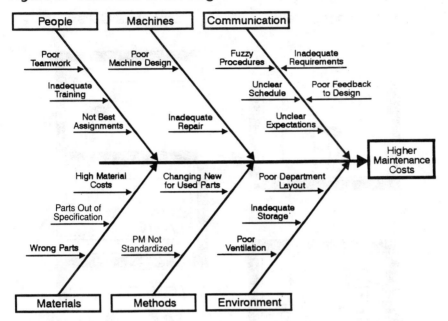

tire sequence of manufacturing operations in one contiguous physical location (cell). Cells are typically designed to perform all of the manufacturing **processes** required for production of a family (or **commodity**) of parts.

Cellular manufacturing typically involves one (or both) of two basic manufacturing floor configurations: the **U-shaped cell** or the **serpentine cell**. The U-shaped cell uses a minimum number of operators (often only one) inside an area where the work moves around the worker(s) on three sides, and the operator is standing inside the "U." This allows the operator to move from position to position with only a few steps and provides the flexibility to perform any combination of three operations without leaving the area. The serpentine cell is more than one U-shaped cell hooked together. This configuration allows for maximum flexibility to increase and decrease operators to account for fluctuation in work volume without reconfiguring the work or physical material flow. See Figure 7.

central line or center line (CL)   The horizontal solid line in the center of a process **control chart** that represents the **central tendency** of the sample values, which (if the process is in a state of control) may be directly or indirectly employed to assess a population **parameter**.

***Figure 7.* Cellular manufacturing.**

U-Shaped Cells   Serpentine Cells

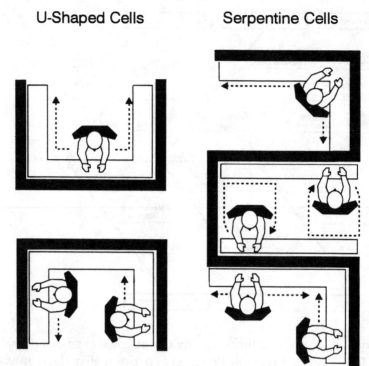

central tendency Measures that describe the scores, values, or observations that occur most often in the data set and/or the location of the center of the data set respective to the data set involved. Measures of central tendency include the **mean**, **median**, and **mode**.

CEO/general manager's role in TQM In TQM implementations, the primary activities of the chief executive officer or general manager. These include the (1) **leadership** of the ongoing TQM meetings of executive management, (2) provision of strategic direction for the overall TQM effort, (3) provision of all required resources in support of TQM implementation, and (4) the highest-level **accountability** for success.

1. **Leadership** should include development of a **vision** of future operations and **motivation** of the work force to attain that vision.
2. *Strategic direction* involves the creation of policies, standard practices, and process-oriented management organization structures for deployment of those policies and practices in support of attain-

ing the vision of future operations. It is based on a strategic plan
and analysis.

3. *Resources* include people, equipment, training, and budget for mis-
cellaneous tools and improvements. They may even involve capital expenditures for facility alterations or consulting fees.

4. *Accountability* involves the establishment of appropriate and measurable **goals** and **objectives** and performance.

certification, ISO 9000   Third-party registration agencies' acknowledg-
ment that an organization or specific company site has met one of three
specific standards of the **International Standards Organization**. Certification is performed in order to create an objective level of assurance that
the specified organization can perform in accordance with specific **quality**
standards, especially when the standards are cited as contractual requirements for suppliers. Generally, the assurance of having met these requirements is called *registration* in North America and *certification* in Europe.
International standards, and particularly international quality standards
such as those represented by **ISO 9000**, are an important contribution to
the TQM environment because they provide an objective measurement
standard by which potential suppliers and partners may be measured.
(ISO 9000 differs significantly from other quality measures because ISO
9000 focuses on the ability to perform to standards that may be outlined
in a contract, whereas credentials such as the **Malcolm Baldrige National
Quality Award** and the **Deming Prize** focus on **continuous improvement**
and world-class quality standing.)

The two basic phases of ISO 9000 registration are:

1. Creating and documenting a quality system (evidenced by a quality manual or master manual) that meets the criteria outlined in a
specific ISO 9000 standard.

2. Certification of compliance to the selected standard by a third-
party registrar. The registrar **audits** the applicant's quality system
to determine whether the system is adequate and is being com-
plied with throughout the organization. Registration, once
awarded, is renewed periodically (typically every two or three
years).

The central point of contact for ISO 9000 registration is the
American Society for Quality Control. The **Registrar Accreditation**

Board is a nonprofit subsidiary of ASQC, and this group is responsible for accrediting registrars and publishing a directory of them.

change   A modification or transformation. In a TQM environment, two kinds of change are required: cultural change and process change. Cultural change is reflected in the attitudes and behavior of employees, but is based on an underlying change in the values used to run the company. (See **company culture** and **organizational values**.) These values are effected by everyone, but for the most part, they are generated by top management and flow down through the organization. They represent the character of the company, just as individual value sets reflect the character of that individual. Examples of commonly stated values include "The **customer** is always right" and "Our people are our most important asset." Many companies involved in TQM embrace values that align with ideals like the ones expressed in **Deming**'s **14 points**.

Process changes involve altering the inputs, activities, and/or outputs of a **process** to gain **efficiencies**. These efficiencies are generally experienced as **cycle time** (or throughput time) reductions, labor hour reductions, **quality** improvements, or general cost reductions (such as floor space reductions or inventory reductions). Other reasons for initiating process changes include safety enhancements, **accountability** improvements, and the attainment of uniformity of processes between sister companies and organizations within a company. Process changes are generally achieved by documenting existing process flows, **brainstorming** to identify potential solutions, selecting and implementing the most appropriate solution, and documenting the changes. Note that there is often an interaction between cultural and process change, and process change (improvement) can sometimes be inhibited by cultural aspects. In general, cultural change is far more difficult to achieve than process change.

change management   The management of **change** in a TQM organization, which generally takes two forms. One form is the management of major change initiatives associated with the TQM implementation itself. This kind of change activity consists of cultural and process changes, as described in **change**. The second type of change management is the continuous, deliberate management of company-wide change to keep abreast of technology, environmental factors, **customer needs**/expectations, and competitors' processes. Described by Duncan in *Manufacturing 2000* (New York: AMACOM, 1994), this process involves continually monitoring both internal and external sources to identify improvement opportunities, analyzing and assimilating the appropriate opportunities, and deploying the results throughout the organization. See also **competitor influences**.

channels of distribution   See **distribution channels**.

characteristic   Any property of an item that distinguishes it from other items. Items usually have many characteristics and can cover products, services, and so forth. In TQM implementations, the characteristics most commonly dealt with are physical characteristics. These include properties such as weight (which yields the characteristic *heaviness*), surface finish (which yields the characteristic *smoothness*), and dimension (which yields the characteristic *size*). See also **critical process characteristics**, **critical product characteristics**, and **external critical characteristic approval and review system**.

chartering a team   A formal **process** that defines the purpose of the project; the measures of success that will be used to assess the project; identification of **team member's role**, **sponsors**, and **stakeholders**; identification of project deliverables; and terms/limits of **empowerment**. Also called *commissioning a team*.

check sheet   A clear, easy-to-use form used in **data collection**. Customized to fit the specific application involved, the check sheet (or tally sheet) is usually made up of potential causes identified in the **cause-and-effect diagram** and is structured in a manner that allows the frequency of occurrences to be recorded for each cause. The check sheet is one of the **seven basic tools of quality**. See Figure 8.

chronic problem   A problem that occurs repeatedly.

CIM   See **computer-integrated manufacturing**.

CIP   See **continuous improvement plan**.

CL   See **central line or center line**.

CNC   See **computer numerically controlled equipment**.

Figure 8. Check sheet.

CHECK SHEET FOR PRINTING ERRORS

BOOK #: _120-0385_   DATE: _5/7/85_

INSPECTOR: _Jane Doe_   LOCATION: _Newhouse Plant_

Defect Type	Check	Subtotal
poor ink coverage	༕ༀ ༕ༀ ///	13
wrong ink	//	2
wrong paper	༕ༀ ༕ༀ ༕ༀ /	16
incorrect cropping	༕ༀ /	6
duplicate pages	༕ༀ ༕ༀ //	12
missing pages	/	1
incorrect folds		0
damaged materials	//	2
	Grand Total	52

REMARKS:

coaching   A style of management, under which the behavior of an employee is changed through education, training, data-based feedback, and advice to improve that employee's work performance. This management style is common in TQM environments, as peers become more involved in each other's performance appraisals and as the rewards and recognition for performance are increasingly **team**-based. This approach contrasts sharply with the traditional autocratic approaches commonly used in more authoritarian, pre-TQM settings. See also **employee involvement**, **reward and recognition system**, and **facilitation**.

comb distribution   A pattern of measured values that, when charted in vertical bars, looks like the edges of a comb. There is a roughly even **distribution** between values with higher and lower values alternating regularly. This phenomenon usually indicates **errors** in the way data are grouped during **histogram** construction. Systematic **bias** in the rounding of values may yield a similar result. See Figure 9.

commissioning a team   See **chartering a team**.

commodity   Any group of parts that requires the same raw materials and the same production resources/equipment to produce them.

commodity analysis   The grouping of parts and/or materials into families based on similarities in raw materials, equipment used in producing the parts, or in rare cases, commonality of supplier and application (i.e., electrical connectors and wire). This technique is most often utilized in **just-in-time** procurement initiatives to improve negotiating leverage, level work loads across groups of production equipment at supplier facilities, and minimize administrative effort required to manage a large, diverse group of purchased items. An important **objective** of performing the commodity analysis is to reduce existing **supplier** bases to one or two suppliers per **commodity**.

commodity-based contracting   Involves the development of contracts with **suppliers** for all (or nearly all) of the parts encompassed within defined **commodities**. A commodity-based contract allows for improved negotiating positions for buyers and results in a mutually beneficial contract when the object of the negotiation moves away from specific parts and delivery quantities toward negotiating for a percentage of the supplier's manufacturing capacity along general machine routings. This approach allows the supplier to be secure over the period of the contract and provides enormous advantages

Figure 9. **Comb distribution.**

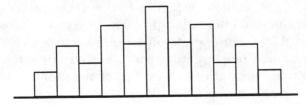

to the buyer in terms of delivery flexibility due to reduced supplier **lead times**.

common causes   Sources of variation that consistently result from a **process** being measured because they are intrinsic to it. These causes may be indigenous to the combination of manpower, methods, materials, or machines used (see **four M's**), or to any one of these factors. These causes will affect individual results as well as more general process measurements.

communication   An exchange of information. The most commonly overlooked, underestimated, and deadly enemy of TQM implementations is poor communication. Communication must be two-way and a high managerial priority. The **daily management board** is a workable tool to promote and improve communication for all organizational levels. Effective communication requires a common language, clarity of expression, and active listening. In a TQM environment, a common language is essential. As people learn new concepts, they often give different meanings to the same terms. A common language is particularly important in defining **customer needs**, **process** requirements, and expected outcomes to precisely define what things mean without resorting to nebulous conceptual jargon. For example, terms like **world class** often give people different impressions and therefore communicate very little useful information. Beyond terminology, it is also important to attain common definitions of the fundamental elements addressed in the TQM implementation. When a particular process is being evaluated, it is extremely important for all parties to have a common understanding of where the process begins and where it ends. Communication should be a primary concern of all TQM implementation leaders as problems are identified, processes are defined, expectations are stated, and improvement **teams** are chartered.

company culture   A company's underlying assumptions, values, and beliefs. These are learned responses to the organization's external survival and internal integration problems, they are shared by employees, and they often operate on an unconscious level—they are taken for granted. Company culture is displayed through individual, team, and organizational behaviors. See **change** for a discussion of cultural change. See also **organizational values**.

comparative and relative importance A reference to the nature of the outcome associated with **customer**/consumer research. The terms are primarily based on the method of data acquisition employed by the researcher.

Comparative importance assessments result from analysis of preference or importance on a one-attribute-at-a-time basis. Likert scales and semantic differential scales are tools commonly used in these assessments. See Figure 10.

Relative importance assessments, on the other hand, result from advanced consumer/customer research methods such as **conjoint analysis**. These techniques provide an assessment of each attribute's importance (or utility) relative to all other features or attributes assessed.

competitive benchmarking See **benchmarking**.

competitor influences Those influences exerted by competitors that are deemed likely to greatly affect the future of a company. These typically include both deliberate and accidental phenomena, which means that they are only somewhat predictable. Examples of deliberate actions include the merger of competing companies and the introduction of new product lines by competitors. Examples of accidental effects include serious **defects** in competitors' products that significantly affect their market share and natural disasters that severely impact the competitors' production capability or capacity. Competitor influences are an important element for consideration by strategic planners and in competitive **benchmarking** activities. See also **market share, importance of**.

compound document exchange (CDE) The electronic exchange of documents containing more than one of the following elements: graphics-, text-, audio-, and video-based data. CDE is an important

Figure 10. **Comparative and relative importance assessment scale.**

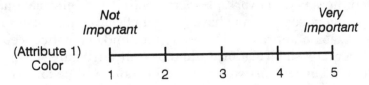

element in the development of effective ways to use the information superhighway. The most common standard used for CDE in future business environments is likely to be computer-aided acquisition and logistics support (CALS).

computer-aided design (CAD)   The use of computers to design products, typically in place of the traditional drawing board, pencil, and vellum or paper. CAD systems became a widespread design tool in the 1970s and have evolved through the 1980s and early 1990s into tools that can produce not only two-dimensional drawings, but also three-dimensional *wire frame* views and shaded three-dimensional models that can be rotated in simulation on screen in real time. Along with enhanced capabilities has come the need for increased computing power, and the developments in CAD software have closely followed the power and speed evolution of computer hardware.

computer-aided process planning (CAPP)   A system typically consisting of part descriptions, manufacturing **process** information, tooling information, and in some cases, labor standards information. The purpose of these systems is to gain **efficiencies** in the development of manufacturing processes. CAPP systems can be useful on a part-by-part basis, but are especially useful when applied to part families or **commodities**.

computer-integrated manufacturing (CIM)   An approach to manufacturing management that focuses on shared information via common databases. It may be viewed simply as the use of computers and information technology to integrate and automate manufacturing **processes** and the processes that support manufacturing. Integration in this context means that all of the information needed to perform any process in the enterprise that is generated by or held anywhere within the enterprise is immediately and constantly available through automated linkages. In the early years of computer-integrated manufacturing research, CIM was thought to require a single common database for the entire enterprise. As technology has evolved, however, networks, servers, and related information technology system components have offered effective alternatives to the single database approach. However, the fundamental concept of a fully integrated information technology infrastructure in any business operation remains valid and will continue to be an extremely important tool for businesses in order to remain competitive throughout the foreseeable future.

computer numerically controlled (CNC) equipment Equipment, usually manufacturing equipment such as metal punches and lathes, controlled directly by computer through a symbolic language. Types of CNC equipment include robots, automated guided vehicles, and any other equipment that may be directed by computer. As factory floor machinery becomes more sophisticated, the skills and technical sophistication of operators must increase as well. Through the balance of the 1990s, the application of CNC equipment will be an important factor in staffing decisions, and will present new challenges and opportunities in terms of process **control**. Also sometimes called *computerized numerical control* equipment.

concurrent engineering The simultaneous design of products and their associated life-cycle management **processes**, including manufacturing, **distribution**, and even obsolescence-related disposition activities. Participants in concurrent engineering **teams** often include design engineering, manufacturing engineering, **quality assurance**, procurement, distribution, marketing, and even **supplier** personnel. Concurrent engineering has been embraced as a means to reduce **cycle-to-market** and the development-related financial risk. When done effectively, it also ensures that all **customer needs** are consistently and effectively met through the design process. See also **configuration management**.

configuration management The effective **control** of product structures. Configuration management is an extremely important aspect of **concurrent engineering** and manufacturing operations since it substantially affects the **efficiency** of manufacturing operations, inventory levels, and **customer satisfaction**. Properly configured products minimize redundancy and non-value-added labor in manufacturing operations. They also prevent ordering expensive product components earlier than necessary to support manufacturing sequences. In addition, properly configured products ensure that **customers** receive exactly what they ordered. As we move through the last half of the 1990s, configuration management will be a fertile area for the application of expert systems and knowledge-based systems. Companies with excellent configuration management will certainly be perceived by their customers as having **quality** levels that are superior to their competitors.

conformance   Concordance with predetermined requirements, meaning that the product or service has met the relevant **specification** and contract requirements.

conformance quality   The consistency with which each unit of product delivered, or each aspect of service provided, is faithful to the design **specification** and relevant **target value**.

conjoint analysis   An advanced and statistically based approach to the assessment of **customer** or consumer preferences associated with attribute, feature, or element analysis for a product or service. In this type of research, fractional factorial diagrams (often of the classification called *orthogonal arrays*) are used to create a series of product or prototype descriptions. The descriptions are then assessed by a **sample** of customers or consumers who rank the descriptions from most to least desirable. The **mean** rank values are subsequently used in an **analysis of variance** to generate utility indices that provide an indication of the relative importance of the attributes or features assessed. Virtually any product or service may be assessed in this fashion. See also **comparative and relative importance**.

conscious error   See **operator-controllable error**.

consensus   The understanding and commitment of an entire group on a concept, approach, or strategic direction or intent. Achieving consensus among members is essential to effective **team** operations. Consensus, however, does not imply (as popularly portrayed) total agreement, but total support. As Margaret Thatcher said, "Consensus [referring to the goal of 100% agreement] is the abrogation of leadership." There are several techniques that may be used to achieve consensus. Two of the most popular tools are **brainstorming** and the **nominal group technique**.

  Often, some individual group members remain privately unconvinced that the approach adopted by the entire group is the optimum solution, but agree to go along with the group decision. This situation leads to an apparent consensus but not a true consensus and is often dangerous because these group members have a way of undermining progress during downstream implementation activities. Team **leaders** and **facilitators** should be wary of this condition and make every effort to remedy it through education, persuasion, or replacement of **team members**.

constraint management A process of identifying constraints or bottlenecks in manufacturing operations, then making adjustments in the **process** to prevent recurrence of each constraint. As knowledge-based systems are more frequently applied, expert systems will handle constraint management as a normal part of administrative oversight functions. The principles of constraint management apply in almost any business.

consultant's role in TQM The part that consultants play in effective TQM implementation. The primary role of the (external) consultant is to bring **profound knowledge** (**Deming**) to the organization attempting to develop a TQ culture. As implied by Deming, a group of people in a pit cannot dig themselves out of that pit. They may dig harder, or faster, but the pit simply gets deeper. The role of the (external) consultant is, in essence, to bring the ladder and to train the people in the organization (pit) to use it on their own.

Roles, in the context of the provision of profound knowledge, where consultants can be extremely valuable in TQM implementations, include planning of the overall TQM implementation activity; general TQM training, especially for initial implementation teams and executive management; specific technical training for implementation **team members**; and facilitating initial team meetings where team building and objectivity are critical.

continuous data Data that are quantifiable, measurable, and can be classified according to some continuum such as ounces, meters, or feet. See also **interval data**, **ratio data**, and **variable data**.

continuous improvement The improvement of products, **processes**, and/or services on an ongoing basis. The gains made through continuous improvement activities are generally incremental, small-step improvements, as contrasted with more dramatic and sweeping improvements typically associated with initiatives such as **policy deployment**. In Japan, the continuous improvement process is often called **kaizen**.

continuous improvement plan (CIP)   A plan designed to incorporate the philosophy of continuously improving every **process** and product into the culture of a company. (See **company culture**.) The plan should outline specific **training** and improvement guidelines. The training included in this plan should prepare participants to seek out **root causes** in **problem solving** and stress **prevention** as opposed to **detection** of **defects**. The plans typically include initial awareness training; more detailed problem solving and TQM tool training; initiation of improvement activities; and the monitoring of regular, ongoing improvement activities, including **reward and recognition systems** to reinforce the application of **continuous improvement** throughout the company. See also **detection vs. prevention**.

contracting, commodity-based   See **commodity-based contracting**.

control   An approach to **process** quality that involved the identification of changes in processes due to special (external) causes of **variability** so as to allow the process owner(s) to take appropriate action. (See **special causes**.) In those cases where the special causes of variation are positive, the process owner(s) attempts to make those effects common to the process. In the event that the special cause of variation is negative, the process owner(s) has the responsibility to eliminate the effects and take those actions necessary to prevent their recurrence. These actions are accomplished through the use of process **control charts** (called Shewhart charts in select applications) and may be applied to critical quality characteristics (**satisfiers**), **defects**, or **defective** unit monitoring. Further, the (statistical) control process may be utilized in conjunction with product quality, product performance, service, administrative, and delivery applications.

control chart   A chart containing **control limits** and a plot of statistical values from a series of **samples** or **subgroups**. (See also **upper control limit** and **lower control limit**.) The chart also contains a **center line** to help detect **trends** away from the process center and toward either control limit. The control chart is one of the **seven basic tools of quality**. See Figure 11.

control group   A group of subjects matched with an experimental group, but not subjected to the action being taken in the experiment. The control group is used to more clearly demonstrate the effects of

Figure 11. **Control chart elements.**

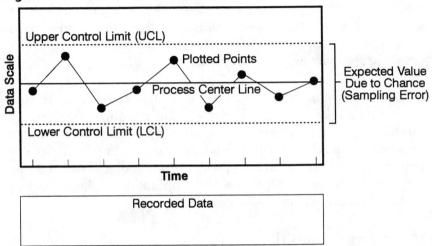

the treatment applied by contrasting its condition at the end of the experiment with the condition of the experimental group. Since the experimental group is exposed to some treatment and the control group is not, a common assumption is that the differences in the condition of these two groups at the end of the experiment result from the application of the treatment to one group and not the other.

control limits   The boundaries (represented as horizontal dashed lines) on a **control chart** that define the limits within which statistical values calculated on **subgroups** of data will naturally fluctuate when the **process** is in a state of **control**. When in a state of control, a process is influenced only by **common causes** of **variability**, and as such, the process output is stable and predictable and should reveal only a random pattern of variation through time. The observation of points outside the control limits, or of specific (nonrandom) patterns of variability within the control limits, is an indication of the presence of **special causes** of variability, and in such cases, the process is identified as out of control. Control limits are calculated using (historical) process data and are not associated with **specification limits** (or **tolerances**) or desired levels of performance. See **lower control limit** and **upper control limit**. See also **in-control process** and **out-of-control process**.

convergence, sequential   The combination of two or more technologies over a substantial period of time, resulting in a third type of technology or a new field of technology application. For example, composites technology, which had already been in fairly widespread use for many years, converged with the relatively new field of robotics. A resulting application technology is composite robot components. See also **convergence, simultaneous**.

convergence, simultaneous   The combination of two or more technologies within a relatively short period of time, resulting in a third type of technology or a new field of technology application. For example, the development of highly pure plastics converged with the development of fiber optics technology, which came along about the same time. A resulting materials technology application is plastic fiber optics. See also **convergence, sequential**.

COQ   See **cost of quality**.

corrective action   The act of implementing a solution that removes a **root cause** and lessens a known problem.

correlation coefficient   A value that represents the relationship between two or more variables. These indices may indicate independence between the variables measured, or may suggest a relationship, positive or negative, between the elements measured, although the presence of a relationship does not guarantee that a causal association exists.

cost drivers   Aspects of an activity that generate cost. These elements are usually identified within an environment of **activity-based costing**, during a process called process value analysis (PVA). There are two categories of cost drivers: primary (highly qualitative) and volume-based (highly quantitative). The costs associated with volume-driven factors are usually readily identified within the cost accounting system, whereas those associated with the primary drivers are not.

Primary Cost Drivers include:
- **communication**
- availability (of tools, material, data, and people)
- complexity
- redundancy
- priority
- timeliness

Volume-Based Cost Drivers Include the Number of:

- **inspections**
- material moves
- orders
- shortages

- transactions
- setups
- receipts

costing, activity-based   See **activity-based costing**.

cost/schedule/quality relationship   A widely held (but incorrect) axiom in pre-TQM environments that there is a fixed relationship between these elements and that an increase in any one of the factors would generate a corresponding increase in the other two areas. In reality, increased **quality** levels lower cost and improve schedule performance. A fundamental flaw in the logic that produced the axiom was the definition used for the word *quality*. Managers believed that quality could be "inspected in," which merely increases cost and lengthens schedules to improve **process** yields. Quality is produced by adequate process **controls**, preventing **defects**, and reducing downstream **inspection**, rework, and scrap costs.

cost of quality (COQ)   A term used to describe the total cost associated with the **quality** of products or services. Costs of quality include **prevention costs**, **appraisal costs**, and internal and external failure costs. (See **internal failure costs** and **external failure costs**.) These costs are usually much greater than those immediately recognized because they include systems costs and personnel costs usually considered fixed. Among the least recognized elements are engineering changes resulting from poor-quality designs and customer relations costs associated with poor-quality products and services.

cost-price model   An equation used to describe the relationship between product cost and the price of that same product. In pre-TQM environments, this equation is often thought to be: Cost + Desired Profit = Price. In TQM environments, the equation is more correctly defined as: Market Price − Cost = Profit. This approach shifts the emphasis from a producer-based emphasis to a **customer focus** and recognizes that success will hinge on reducing cost from market price through process **control**, **stability**, and improvement.

costs, appraisal   See **appraisal costs**.

counseling A management style and technique that is supportive of the employee, assisting the employee in identifying and working through personal and professional problems that are adversely affecting job performance.

covariate See **independent variable**.

C_p A statistical index value that reveals the capability potential of a **process**. This index takes into account only the **variability** of a process relative to the **specifications** or **tolerances**. The C_p index is a "bigger is better" index with a value of 1.0, indicating minimum acceptable capability, although some organizations require at least 1.33. C_p values less than 1.0 indicate that the process lacks the potential to be capable. This index should only be calculated for processes running in a state of **control**. See **in-control process**. See also **process capability** for a full discussion and computational information.

C_{pk} A statistical index value that reveals the capability of a **process**, which takes into account not only process **variability** (as does the C_p index), but also considers the degree to which the process average is centered between (bilateral) **specification limits**. In its original form, C_{pk} is specifically associated with the percentage of individual observations expected to be **out of specification** on the side of the distribution where the capability is the worst. C_{pk} is at its maximum value (which is equal to C_p) when the process average is exactly halfway between specification limits. As with C_p, this index should not be calculated unless the process has been documented to be running in a state of **control**. See **in-control process**. See also **process capability** for a full discussion and computational information.

C_{pm} A statistical index value which, like C_{pk}, reveals the capability of a **process**. However, unlike C_{pk}, which assesses capability as a function of both **variability** and the degree to which the process average is centered between (bilateral) **specification limits**, C_{pm} assesses capability as a function of variability and the degree to which the process average deviates away from the designated ideal or **target value**. C_{pm} takes on its largest value when the process average is equal to the target value or **nominal value** (N_o). As with C_p and C_{pk}, C_{pm} should not be calculated unless the process has been documented to be running in a state of **control**. See **in-control process**. See also **process capability** for a full discussion and computational information.

CPM See **critical path method**.

CQA See **customer quality assurance**.

criterion measure A method or scale by which a dependent (or re-sponse) variable is quantitatively or qualitatively assessed. For exam-ple, the **dependent variable** in an experiment might be identified as "metal can quality." This dependent variable, however, might pos-sess numerous **characteristics** to be measured, analyzed, and bal-anced within a single experiment. Trim height, axial load, metal ex-posure, and the presence of voids might constitute the criterion measures associated with the dependent variable of "metal can qual-ity" for a given experiment. If only one criterion measure exists, the dependent variable and criterion measure are typically the same quantity.

critical mass The number of people in any organization who must be actively involved in a transformation to assure that the **change** achieves long-term sustainability.

critical path method (CPM) A technique for identifying all of the activities within a **process**, along with their sequences and interde-pendencies. The longest (in terms of time) chain of activities that must occur in sequence (cannot be done in parallel) within a process is the critical path of that process. The identification of the critical path is a subset of the activities performed as a part of the **program evaluation and review technique**. Identifying the critical path in any process is essential in reducing the throughput time for materials produced through that process. Identifying the critical path in a manufacturing process typically involves these steps:

1. Identify all of the activities in the process.
2. Beginning with the last activity performed in the process, work your way backward through the process, identifying which activities must be completed before the one you are reviewing may be started.
3. Document the dependencies. This is usually done with circles

depicting the activities and arrows between the circles depicting the interrelationships.

4. Identify and document the throughput times associated with
   each activity, labeling the circles with their respective
   throughput times.
5. Sum the total throughput times for each sequence spanning
   the first through the last activity.
6. Identify the chain of activities that represents the longest total
   throughput time, based on step 5. This chain of activities is
   the critical path. See Figure 12.

critical process characteristics   Process **characteristics** or variables
such as temperature, pressure, feed, and run speed that are shown
to have a significant and important effect on an in-process or end-of-
line critical product variable **satisfier** or **dissatisfier**. Importance is
assessed on the basis of the calculation of the amount of **variability**
or influence that the process characteristic explains as related to the
process variable. This degree of importance may only be assessed as
a result of a designed experiment.

Critical process variables may also be categorized as first-, sec-
ond-, or third-order characteristics. First-order variables are those
that directly impact a product characteristic. Second-order process
variables are those that directly affect a first-order process variable,
thereby indirectly affecting the product characteristic in question.
Third-order process characteristics are critical influences as they directly impact critical second-order variables.

Figure 12. Critical path method.

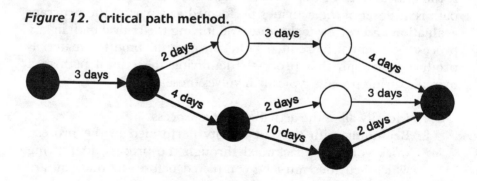

NOTE: The critical path is highlighted, requiring a total of 19 days.

critical product characteristic A quality **characteristic** (or **satisfier**) that is significant and important to the **customer** as related to form, fit, function, use, or safety as associated with the part or product supplied. These characteristics will, at a minimum, possess a nominal and/or **target value**, and at least one **specification** that will describe the minimum acceptability level of the product, part, or component. Typically, the **nominal value** and/or **target value** and specification(s) are and should be based on engineering design, testing, and analysis. See Figure 13.

cross-functional team A special-purpose group composed of persons from different areas (cutting through the organization horizontally rather than vertically) that has been commissioned to address a specific issue or subject.

cultural change See **change**.

culture (company or corporate) See **company culture**.

curve, bell-shaped See **bell-shaped curve** and **normal distribution**.

Figure 13. Critical product characteristics.

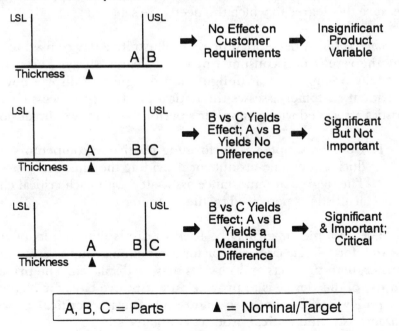

customer, external   An individual (or group of individuals) outside the organization who are the recipients of products or services of that organization. Examples include product consumers, clients, local communities, and the general public. See also **customer, internal**.

customer, internal   An individual (or group of individuals) inside an organization who is the recipient of a product or service produced within that same organization. See also **customer, external**.

customer delight   The pleasure customers get when the delivered product or service meets their needs or requirements and exceeds their expectations.

customer expectations   See **expectations, customer**.

customer feedback   See **feedback, customer**.

customer focus   Constant awareness of **customer needs**, and a consistent effort to satisfy and exceed those needs. Adequate customer focus requires that **customers** and the needs of those customers be discretely identified and addressed and provides the opportunity to measure the degree to which the needs are satisfied.

customer map   A perceptual map; an illustrative device used to display the results of a consumer/market research study. The map is generally organized in a configuration designed to display how an individual **customer** assesses the critical product or process characteristics associated with a **supplier's** performance in two dimensions:

1. How the supplier is performing relative to competitors producing the same product or providing the same service
2. The degree of importance associated with each critical characteristic as perceived by the customer

The customer map may be used to display the results of such research for a single customer or for a common group of customers. Further, both products and services may be displayed. The primary end use of this device is to provide an illustrative basis for planning and **policy deployment**. See Figure 14. See also **critical process characteristic** and **critical product characteristic**.

Figure 14. Sample configuration for a customer (perceptual) map.

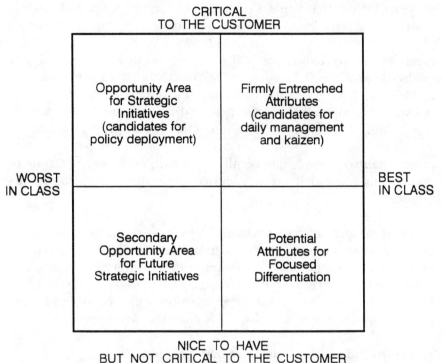

CRITICAL
TO THE CUSTOMER

Opportunity Area
for Strategic
Initiatives
(candidates for
policy deployment)

Firmly Entrenched
Attributes
(candidates for
daily management
and kaizen)

WORST
IN CLASS

BEST
IN CLASS

Secondary
Opportunity Area
for Future
Strategic Initiatives

Potential
Attributes for
Focused
Differentiation

NICE TO HAVE
BUT NOT CRITICAL TO THE CUSTOMER

customer mapping process   A basic **customer** research approach that is also known as *customer window, voice of the customer,* and *listening to the customer*. In this process, customer representatives are interviewed or surveyed in order to assess their perceptions of the products and services of a particular **supplier**. Additional information gleaned from this process may also include customer assessments of what the supplier might consider improving. The outcome of this research approach, which is most functional for **dissatisfier** analysis, may be the development of a perceptual or **customer map**. See also **critical process characteristic** and **critical product characteristic**.

customer needs   An important feature of a company's strategy and **quality** system. Customer needs help to define *quality,* since quality products conform to customer needs, translated through the business to mean **conformance** to design specifications. Customer needs are identified in several ways, including market surveys, analysis of buying patterns, and the **Delphi technique**. They are defined and translated into specific business actions through **quality function deployment**. Note that while a customer needs a product within specifications, the same customer wants a product at the optimum target.

customer quality assurance (CQA)   A supporting element of **total quality assurance**. The components of customer quality assurance include advanced quality planning, **customer** plant integration, tracking the voice of the customer, and new product introduction/ marketing. See Figure 15. See also **customer mapping process**.

customer satisfaction   The result of meeting **customer** needs or requirements when delivering a service or product. See also **dissatisfaction**.

customer satisfaction measurement   A process, typically owned by executive management, in which **customer satisfaction** data are continuously gathered (through **customer** surveys, interviews, sales force feedback, telemarketing feedback, etc.) and analyzed to identify both levels and trends of customer satisfaction with the organization's products and services. See also **survey-feedback process**.

customer window   See **customer mapping process**.

cycle-to-market   The time required from concept to initial product delivery, including all design, production, and **distribution** activities.

cycle time   In cycle reduction activities, the elapsed time of a **process** from beginning to end. This elapsed time includes both value-added and non-value-added activity. In machine operations, cycle time is more accurately defined as the time required for the machine to cycle through one recurring sequence of activities. See also **value-added analysis**, **concurrent engineering**, and **lead time**.

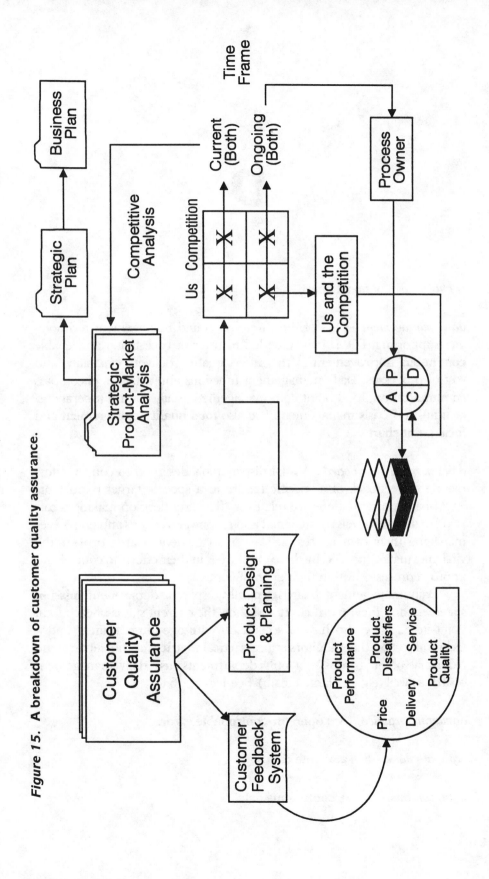

Figure 15. A breakdown of customer quality assurance.

D

D-chart   See **demerit chart**.

daily management   One of the three integrated management technologies supporting TQM. It is intended to prevent backsliding and enable **continuous improvement** in the safety, **quality**, delivery capability, and cost of **processes**. Daily management functions and activities encompass **communication**, focal point item management, daily control (operations/tactical), and crisis management. See also **total quality management** and **focal point chart**.

daily management board   Visual display tools designed to convey information or feedback of a specific nature to a specific target population. TQM-based organizations are relatively "flat" and decision making is carried out at lower levels by informed and **empowered** teams and employees managing their own processes. Daily management boards provide the vital information needed by these employees in their efforts to control and improve processes within their **span of control**.

Daily management boards typically display a department **mission statement** and **focal point chart** and show the current status of each focal point item. They also have a section on **employee involvement** and a technical section that monitors critical **tactical metrics** for the department. Note that other groups, not only departments, use daily management boards as well (e.g., a plant, a team). See Figure 16.

damaging practice   See **operator-controllable error**.

data, attribute   See **attribute data**.

data, continuous   See **continuous data**.

48

Figure 16. **Examples of daily management boards.**

Board Name	Purpose	Target Population
Department Daily Management Board	To convey feedback information on the progress of the organization toward achieving critical targets and goals and continuously improving performance	Members of the department
Project Management Board	To explain, describe, and monitor the purpose and progress of a critical project	Employees affected by the project and those implementing it
Scheduling or Production Control Board	To describe the sequence, timing, or provide critical information concerning the scheduling of changeovers, assignments, deployments, etc.	Employees affected by or performing the scheduled activities
Workstations	To display critical information needed to control and monitor a process or operation (control charts, SOPs, check sheets)	Workers running the process or operation
Kanbans	To control the flow of material through a series of operations or processes	Workers and supervisors running the area

data collection   The gathering of data to identify methods of, and progress toward, **process** improvement. A sound strategy for data collection includes the answers to these questions:

1. What do we plan to learn from the data?
2. What specific data are needed?
3. What specific metrics will be needed to document the data?
4. At what points in which specific process must the data be collected?
5. What sampling methods will be used?
6. Who will be responsible for collecting the data and how frequently?
7. How will the data be reported, to whom, by whom, and how frequently?

Gathering too much data and gathering the wrong data can be counterproductive. Faulty analysis of even flawlessly gathered data can be misleading. However, good, solid data-gathering strategies and tactics are essential to monitoring and improving process and system health.

data encryption standards (DES)   Standards utilized to secure the data communicated between two or more computers or telecommunications devices. DES devices are typically comprised of a single computer chip used for encoding and decoding that is installed at each end of a communication line.

data interchange   See **electronic data interchange**.

data sharing   See **advanced procurement technology**.

decision matrix   A matrix-based chart used to assign relative priorities among **corrective actions**. Problems are listed on the Y axis of the chart, and potential solutions are listed on the X axis, at the top of the chart. Each corrective action (potential solution) is then rated within vertical cells of the matrix corresponding to each problem. Ratings for potential solutions are summed to assign relative priority. See also **comparative and relative importance**.

decision support systems (DSS)   Systems (typically software) designed and deployed to support human decision making in some technical area. Decision support systems are constantly growing in application base, sophistication, and importance. They will eventually take over much of the redundant analysis in low-level decision making in business organizations. Initial applications, which are likely to become flagships for future development work, include inventory planning and management, sales and market analysis, and transportation routing activity. See also **artificial intelligence**.

defect   **Nonconformity** to **specification**, including any **failure** to satisfy an intended use. (See also **conformance**.) A part may have any number of defects. Defects may be categorized as:

- *Critical*. Capable of resulting in serious injury or loss of life.
- *Serious*. Capable of resulting in catastrophic economic loss.
- *Major*. Capable of resulting in product or service **failure** under normal usage conditions.
- *Minor*. Capable of resulting in minor problems during the normal, intended use of the product or service, and/or some economic loss.

defective   Term used to identify any product or service that fails to conform to **specifications** and/or does not satisfy its intended purpose or function. See also **conformance**.

degrees of freedom (df)   Generally, the freedom of scores to vary. This term also refers to the number of observations that can vary independently of one another. Often, conditions exist that impose restrictions such that the number of degrees of freedom is less than the number of scores in the **sample**. In **random samples**, the degrees of freedom are equal to the sample size minus one.

delight   See **customer delight**.

Delphi technique   A subjective forecasting method that involves the use of a panel of experts brought to group **consensus** on the most likely course of a specified subject. In the Delphi process, each individual expert develops his or her own forecast on the subject and the forecasts are submitted anonymously to a group **facilitator**. The facilitator reviews the forecasts and prepares a summary report, which is returned to all the Delphi experts. The experts then review the summary report and prepare a revised forecast based on the summary. The process is repeated until the forecasts converge.

demand elasticity   Term used to describe an environment where market demand for a product or service substantially increases when the price of the product or service is reduced. When a price decrease results in a sales increase (measured as a percentage) greater than the price reduction (again measured as a percentage), the demand is considered *elastic*.

demerit chart (D-chart)   A type of **control chart** using **attribute data** that show the number of **defective** units weighted by their importance. See Figure 17.

Deming cycle   See **PDCA cycle** and **Shewhart/Deming cycle**.

Deming Prize   A **quality** prize awarded annually to selected organizations that, according to award guidelines, successfully applied companywide **quality control** based on **statistical quality control** and have demonstrated a commitment to maintain quality systems. The

Figure 17. **Demerit chart (D-chart).**

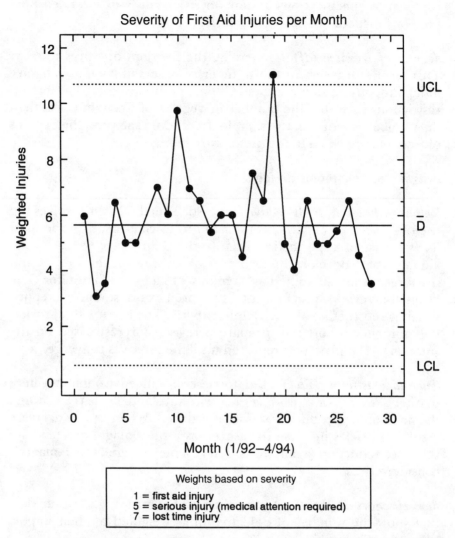

award is named after **W. Edwards Deming**, though its criteria are not directly aligned with Deming's teachings. The three separate award categories are the Deming Application Prize, the Deming Prize for Individuals, and the Deming Prize for Overseas Companies. The Deming Prize Committee of the Union of Japanese Scientists and Engineers (JUSE) in Tokyo oversees the award process.

Deming, W. Edwards A renowned **quality** leader, consultant, teacher, and author. Deming shared his knowledge of **statistical quality control** to help the U.S. war effort during World War II and was then sent to Japan in 1946 to help the nation recover from its wartime losses. He authored more than 200 works, including acclaimed books such as *Quality, Productivity, and Competitive Position* and *Out of the Crisis*. Deming's **14 points** still represent a widely respected set of quality management guidelines.

dependent variable The variable affected in an experiment; also called *response variable*. This variable represents the outcome or end condition under study. It is usually the factor that the research is aimed at understanding and/or controlling. Examples of responses (or dependent variables) include trim height, cleanliness, and time to **failure**. Virtually any measurable customer **satisfier** (quality **characteristic**) may be studied as a dependent variable. See also **criterion measure**.

deployment phase See **implementation phase (phase IV)**.

DES See **data encryption standards**.

descriptive statistics Values that describe a **sample** or **subgroup** in terms of **central tendency, dispersion**, and **shape**. See also **parameter**.

design, experimental See **experimental design, design of experiments**, and **basic tools of experimental design**.

design for assembly (DFA) An approach to the design of manufactured products characterized by a deliberate intent and consistent actions to facilitate assembly of the product. This approach usually focuses not only on ease of fit-up and clarity of assembly sequence, but also on minimization of required tools for assembly tasks.

design for disassembly An approach to the design of manufactured products characterized by a deliberate intent and consistent actions to facilitate the disassembly of the product at the end of its useful life. (This is usually done for disposal, remanufacturing, or recycling.)

design for logistics   An approach to the design of manufactured products characterized by a deliberate intent and consistent actions to facilitate the physical handling and **distribution** of the final product through delivery to the end **customer**.

design of experiments (DOE)   A branch of applied statistics in which controlled tests are planned, implemented, and interpreted in order to identify and assess the importance of those factors affecting the value of one or more **parameters** associated with a **dependent (response) variable** or condition. Specifically, a designed experiment is intended to allow the researcher to efficiently manipulate **independent variables** in such a way that effects noted on the dependent (response) variable are correctly attributed and quantified. Methods of manipulation include incorporation, nesting, blocking, **control**, and limitation. In industry, the designed experiment is constructed to maximize the information gained at the minimum time and cost possible, while obtaining internally and externally (i.e., generalizable) valid results. See also **experimental design** and **basic tools of experimental design**.

design quality   Accurate identification of critical quality **characteristics (satisfiers)** and their appropriate **nominal** or **target values** that, if met, will result in optimal product or **process** performance. Optimal performance is defined by stated performance and **reliability** requirements. All stated requirements should directly or indirectly relate to the needs of the **customer**. See also **customer needs**.

design review   A systematic search for design problems conducted at designated intervals throughout the product design process. The purpose of the review is to identify problems, identify alternatives to resolve those problems, and assure performance to **quality**, cost, and schedule milestones, and in so doing, to assure **design quality**. Among the benefits of the design review are:

1. Provision of an organized forum for the discovery and examination of product problems and issues
2. Provision of consistent direction for all working levels and identification of specific responsibilities and assignments
3. Deployment of design and development resources on the most critical problems in order to assure timely resolution

4. Minimization of the potential for a problem to be overlooked
5. Application of the collective experience of all affected functions and departments
6. Enhanced coordination of activities within the design process and with other nondesign activities

design verification Term used to describe a series of tests required to qualify new/modified designs. The tests are compiled in a document called a design verification plan, which is the responsibility of design engineering. The design verification plan is revised as needed to account for **changes** in operational requirements, **customer** expectations, and government regulations. (See also **expectations, customer**.) The plan is developed annually, or as significant changes are made in product design. It covers test specifics, acceptance criteria, **sample sizes**, and completion dates. It also indicates which individuals are responsible for each designated activity.

designer materials A class of new materials that are formulated and constructed to exhibit specific properties in use as part of a product. Composites and other polymers, as well as specially developed metal alloys, are typical representatives of this category of material.

designing in quality vs. inspecting in quality See **detection vs. prevention**.

destructive testing Any form of product testing that renders the product unusable. Most commonly, this type of testing is used to evaluate structural strength and durability. It may involve using the product until its useful life has been exhausted, or even cutting the product in half to evaluate internal **characteristics**. See also **nondestructive testing**.

detection Identifying a nonconformance after it exists.

detection vs. prevention A comparison of two types of quality activities: identifying a nonconformance after it exists (**detection**) versus not permitting it to occur in the first place (**prevention**). One of the most important aspects to understand about TQM is that prevention is far less costly than detection. Process **control** and improvement are the only ways to prevent **defects**. Improving **processes** improves product **quality** levels, and improving processes means reducing variation in those processes around their optimum targets. This makes process control the least costly and most effective method of ensuring quality. See also **nonconformity**, **conformance**, and **prevention costs**.

deviation   Any nonconformance in a product or service from the **specifications** for that product or service. A product may deviate from the stated specification, or nominal position, without being outside of stated **tolerances**. In this case, the product deviates without necessarily being **defective**. See also **nonconformity** and **nominal value**.

df   See **degrees of freedom**.

DFA   See **design for assembly**.

diagram, blueprint   See **specification limits**.

diagram, fishbone   See **cause-and-effect diagram** and **dispersion analysis**.

disassembly   See **design for disassembly**.

discrete data   See **attribute data**.

dispersion   The **distribution** of scores or values within a data set or within a **population** of occurrences.

dispersion analysis   A method of constructing **cause-and-effect diagrams**. The three steps involved in a dispersion analysis are:

1. *Identify the quality **characteristics** to be improved.* These should be primary customer **satisfiers/dissatisfiers**. List them as main branches on a fishbone or **cause-and-effect diagram**. (If participants have difficulty organizing their ideas in this manner, they may start with the standard *manpower, materials, methods,* and *machines* elements common in the **Ishikawa** fishbone diagram. See **four M's**.)

2. *Brainstorm ideas of possible causes of* **defects** *in the quality characteristics designated in step 1.* List them as secondary branches stemming from the main branch categories listed.

3. *Brainstorm all possible causes of the main cause categories listed from step 2.* Show them as minor "twigs" stemming from these secondary branches.

The completed fishbone diagram can then be used in identifying most **common causes** and deploying **corrective action** and defect **prevention** resources in the most fertile areas of opportunity.

dissatisfaction The state one (usually a customer) experiences when his or her expectations are not met. This term is usually used within the context of **customer satisfaction**. When used in this context, customer satisfaction is considered to be a continuum, with dissatisfaction on one extreme of the continuum and **customer delight** on the other extreme. Satisfaction should be viewed as a point of indifference in the middle of the continuum. (*Note*: Many customer satisfaction surveys seek responses to questions or statements on a scale ranging from "very dissatisfied" to "neither satisfied nor dissatisfied" to "very satisfied." Items of this type on a survey do not allow one to determine customer delight.)

dissatisfier Any feature or attribute of a product or service that is not associated with a quality **characteristic (satisfier)**, and if present, represents a deficiency, potentially resulting in scrap, rework, or **customer** complaints. Examples include cracks or voids in product surfaces, invoice errors, and "bugs" in computer programs.

distribution In statistical applications, the pattern that randomly collected data displays when depicted graphically. Types of distributions include **normal**, **binomial**, **skewed**, and **Poisson**. Variations in the **processes** involved generate differences in the distribution of **sample** values that result in these different pattern types.

In manufacturing, this term refers to the methods and activities used to move products from the producer into the marketplace.

distribution channels The primary methods of **distribution** activity used to move products from manufacturers to end users. These include motor carriers, air carriers, water transportation, and rail.

distribution requirements planning (DRP)   The system used to manage warehousing and **distribution** activity, usually considered a module of **manufacturing resource planning** systems. It maintains warehouse and distribution center inventory, monitors transportation and shipping activity, and sometimes includes electronic communication between the factory, distribution centers, and commercial carriers.

distribution types   See **binomial distribution**, **comb distribution**, **exponential distribution**, and **frequency distribution**.

distributive numerical control (DNC)   Machine **control** managed by one or more computers, typically at the machine site itself.

diversification phase   See **networking phase (phase V)**.

DNC   See **distributive numerical control.**

document exchange   See **compound document exchange**.

DOE/DOX   See **design of experiments**.

double Pareto diagram   A special "back-to-back" **Pareto chart** (one of the **seven basic tools of quality**) used to depict and contrast two sets of data, or before-and-after data pertaining to a **process** or system. See Figure 18.

double-peaked distribution   A graph, typically a bar graph, that depicts a distinct "valley" in a range of data, with "peaks" on either side. Most often, this **distribution** indicates two processes are at work in the **population** shown and/or two different sets of data have been tabulated together. Also commonly called a *bimodal distribution*. See Figure 19.

drivers, business   See **business drivers**.

drivers, cost   See **cost drivers**.

DRP   See **distribution requirements planning**.

Figure 18. **Double Pareto diagram.**

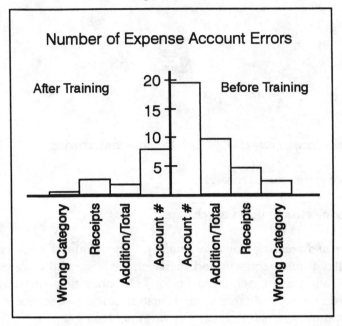

Figure 19. **Bimodal/double-peaked distribution.**

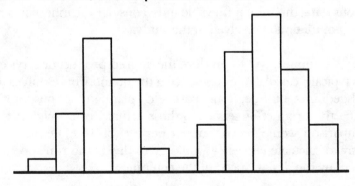

DSS   See **decision support systems**.

duty cycle   (Run time) divided by (run time plus setup time for the operation).

E

economic order quantity (EOQ) See **batch manufacturing**.

ECR See **error cause removal**.

EDI See **electronic data interchange**.

education and training (for total quality) The required knowledge for total quality implementation and management. (See also **training**.) The education and training requirements for TQM operations vary widely depending on the type of environment (manufacturing vs. service, no prior TQM exposure vs. mature **quality** environment, etc.).

effect size The minimum difference or relationship that is desired for detection at selected **Type I** (**alpha**) and **Type II** (**beta**) **error** levels. For **continuous data**, this minimum value must consider the inherent **variability** of the **population(s)** involved in the study.

efficiency Minimum cost to produce the desired product or service. Efficiency is typically calculated by comparing the quantity of resources (labor, materials, equipment time, floor space, etc.) planned for consumption in producing the product or service to those actually consumed. A one-to-one comparison would be considered perfect (or 100%) efficiency. Another way to calculate efficiency would be to divide the run speed of the equipment by the design speed of the equipment.

elasticity See **demand elasticity**.

electronic data interchange (EDI) The exchange of information by electronic means. The combination of computer and communications technology is yielding extremely efficient, effective, and relatively low-cost electronic data exchange methods. These developments support the movement of **TQM** companies toward sharing a great deal of their operating data with **suppliers** and **customers**. (See the *data sharing* discussion in the **advanced procurement technology** listing.) In nearly every major organizational process, electronic data interchange is becoming a central tool for daily operations. In the future, as individual departments are linked to other departments through local area networks (LANs), and those networks are linked to **wide area networks (WANs)**, and the WANs are linked in turn to national and international networks such as Internet, EDI will become absolutely necessary to remain competitive. (See the illustrations shown in the **architecture, information systems** listing.) Among the most popular hardware and software used for EDI in our current environments are computers, modems, fax machines, and telephone lines. However, we are also moving into more common use of microwaves, satellites, infrared light, and a host of other technologies as the capabilities of new materials and software become evident.

employee involvement   A formal, ongoing process (internal to an organization) in which employees regularly and substantively participate in decision making pertaining to the operations within their **span of control**. This involvement may take place through participation on company, plant, or local TQM steering committees; on commissioned **teams** (e.g., quality improvement or problem-solving teams); on sanctioned teams or **natural work groups**; or through an employee **suggestion system**.

In order for employee involvement initiatives to be successful, management must respect the ideas and efforts of the work force. Management must also support the concept of employee involvement by providing a formal structure for the process and deploying resources as required in a responsible manner to incorporate the suggested improvements. Management personnel must also be role models of employee involvement themselves.

employee selection and training   The choosing and preparation of workers to undertake a TQM initiative, which is critical to achieving early success. Employees selected to lead the way in any TQM initiative must be able to deal with the stress that **change** brings, including the criticism of their ideas, skepticism and cynicism from their peers (and sometimes from management), and the need to compromise in order to achieve team **objectives**. Beyond this personality-related element, some fundamental skills will be required of these employees. **Team** building, basic TQM **training**, and specific targeted training as described under **education and training**

(for total quality) are good prerequisites to initiating improvement activities using any employee.

employee suggestion system   See **suggestion systems**.

empowerment   Giving people the power to improve/manage a system or correct an error. However, this brief description can be misleading, and when it is, very destructive. Empowerment means the endowment of power, but the power must be clearly defined, focused, and limited. When a **team** or employees are empowered, they should be chartered to achieve specific **goals** and **objectives**, informed about the amount and types of resources available to them, and told about the time frame involved in their empowerment and the limitations of that power. (See **chartering a team**.) In this way, no one develops unrealistic expectations or feels unnecessarily constrained in achieving the purpose of the empowerment; at the same time, no one should exceed the limitations of his or her formal power. A good rule to remember for this aspect of TQM is the phrase "no unrealistic expectations, no unnecessary constraints, and no excuses." Empowered employees are provided with the knowledge, tools, responsibility, accountability, and authority within their designated **span of control** to be effective decision makers and take appropriate actions within a designated span of control without prior approval. For example, an employee can be empowered to stop production if he or she detects a problem without an immediate resolution.

end-of-line characteristics   Product variables that have been defined by the **customer** as:

- Quality **characteristics** or **satisfiers** that are critical to **processes** or production systems, and
- Measurable at the end of the **supplier's** production process, immediately before shipment or warehousing for future shipment

See also **critical process characteristics** and **critical product characteristics**.

engineering, concurrent   See **concurrent engineering**.

environment and variation   A look at the environment's influence on variation. The environment is a factor contributing to the variation in virtually every **process**, although some processes are less sensitive to environmental factors than others. For example, chemical processes are often very sensitive to temperature and humidity whereas photoelectric processes are more sensitive to light. Generally, when the environment is closely controlled, the effects of these factors are minimal and may be expected to generate only **common causes** of **variability**, producing a **normal distribution** (**bell-shaped curve**) pattern when process output values are plotted.

EOQ   Economic order quantity. See **batch manufacturing**.

error   Act or instance of deviation from unexpected procedures or methods of work that results in **defects**, scrap, rework, waste, injuries, or any non-value-adding natural consequence. See also **value-added analysis**.

error, conscious   See **operator-controllable error**.

error, experimental   See **experimental error**.

error, inadvertent   See **operator-controllable error**.

error, operator-controllable   See **operator-controllable error**.

error, technique   See **operator-controllable error**.

error cause removal (ECR)   A process designed to provide a formal mechanism enhancing employees' ability to communicate problems effectively to management. (See also **communication**.) In the ECR process, employees are provided with simple, one-page forms that are usually made available in wall-mounted boxes at various locations throughout the workplace. An employee removes and completes the form, then returns it to the box. Completed forms are picked up and then acted upon by the appropriate management on a daily basis.

European Foundation for Quality Management   A foundation located in the Netherlands that awards an "all-Europe" **quality** award known as the **European Quality Award**.

European Quality Award, The (TEQA)   An award administered by the European Foundation for Quality Management, which is similar in concept to the **Malcolm Baldrige National Quality Award**, although it differs somewhat in point values by category. To receive this award, a company is required to demonstrate that its commitment to TQM has contributed significantly to the satisfaction of all company **stakeholders**: **customers**, employees, and other holders of an interest in the company.

evergreen system   A term coined by Mahoney and Thor in their book *The TQM Trilogy* (New York: AMACOM, 1994) to describe a methodology for sustainable quality management systems implementation. The *people dimensions* stressed in this system are **leadership**, human resources development, and management. The three fundamental elements of their program include:

1. *Total involvement,* stressing organizationwide participation
2. *Continuous improvement,* emphasizing the ongoing nature of the program
3. **Customer** *orientation,* focusing on the end user's definition of **quality**

excursion analysis   A strategy used to investigate **failures** that can identify a multitude of **root causes**. Excursion analysis should be conducted by the appropriate problem solvers in the organization on all critical failures that impact the organization or the **customers**. Excursion analysis can lead to such root causes as:

- **Processes** that are out of control (see **out-of-control processes**)
- Processes that are not capable
- Equipment failures
- Incoming material **defects**
- Poor **design quality**
- Environmental effects
- **Operator-controllable errors**
- Management-controllable errors
- Management system failures

executive's role in TQM   A role of strategy development, progress monitoring, and macro-level project management. Executive management constantly assesses the gaps between current and desired future states, and steers the TQM efforts in directions best suited to filling the largest gaps. Outputs from the executive level activities include:

1. *A business architecture.* Includes identified **business drivers**, **business processes**, process performance metrics, and a **resource infrastructure**.
2. *A strategic plan.* Includes all areas defined in the **business architecture**, a future state **vision** of all major business processes, and specific strategic targets associated with each area and process.
3. *A high-level improvement strategy.* Includes specific targets, **team** structures to address each improvement area, improvement activity time lines, and a formal TQM program management structure.

expectations, customer   The expectations of a customer that are either satisfied or dissatisfied over the life cycle of the product or service. Typically, a customer must believe that the product or service will satisfy his or her need before buying it and satisfies the same need while using it. Finally, the customer must be satisfied with service responsiveness and effectiveness when the product fails. These expectations are actually groupings of more specific expectations in each phase of product or service life, with some of the specific expectations listed below:

1. Pre-sale customer expectations:
   A. Clear **specifications** relating to the perceived need
   B. Clear compliance with all applicable safety and usage regulations
   C. Clearly defined performance and reliability **characteristics**
2. Post-sale customer expectations:
   A. On-schedule receipt of product or service
   B. Full operability and inclusion of all components at time of delivery
   C. Freedom from **defects**
   D. User-friendliness
   E. **Reliability** and ease of maintenance and repair

3. Customer expectations at the end of the product or service's useful life:
   A. Economical repair or replacement
   B. Ease and low cost of disposal
   C. In some cases, *upgradability* to new technology

experimental design   The process by which factors are selected for study and deliberately varied in a controlled manner, in order to observe the effects of these actions. The designation of a particular plan for assigning subjects or experimental units to experimental conditions, which may also include statistical analysis of the resulting data. See also **basic tools of experimental design** and **design of experiments**.

experimental error   A measure of all uncontrolled and/or unexplained sources of variation that affects a particular score. Also called *unexplained variation*.

expert systems   See **artificial intelligence**.

exponential distribution   A continuous random variable with the following form:

$$y = \frac{1}{\mu} e^{-x/\mu}$$

where μ is the population **mean** or **mean time between failures**.
   While the **normal distribution** reflects an area of 50% above and below μ, the exponentially distributed **population** has 36.8% above and 63.2% below the average (μ). Examples of **characteristics** described by the exponential distribution include loading patterns for selected structural members and **failure** times for complex equipment. See Figure 20.

external critical characteristic approval and review system   One component of the **supplier quality assurance** system model that relates to the ongoing maintenance of a critical **characteristic** profile, including nominal/target and **specification** control and review systems as associated with all purchased materials. See Figure 21.

Figure 20. **Exponential distribution.**

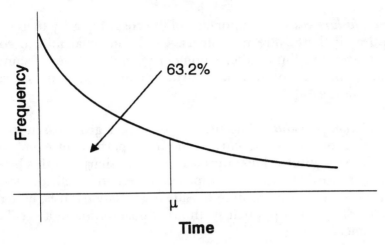

Figure 21. **Breakdown of elements associated with the external critical characteristic approval and review system.**

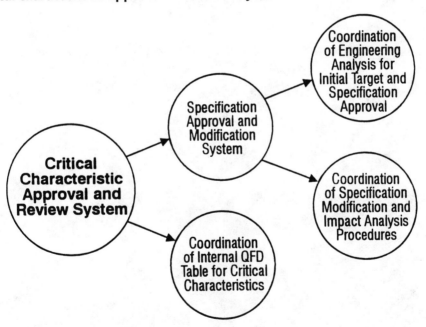

external customer   See **customer, external**.

external failure costs   Components of the **cost of quality** that would disappear if there were no **defects**. Unlike **internal failure costs**, these defects are found after shipment to the customer. Examples include complaint adjustment, returned material, warranty charges, and allowances.

extrapolation planning   The practice of setting **goals** based on extrapolating or projecting current business performance improvements into the future. This approach contrasts sharply with a **benchmarking** process in that the extrapolation method is oblivious to best practices or any comparison to outside organizations. It is, nonetheless, one of the most popular methods of goal setting in a pre-TQM environment.

facilitation The **leadership** of a **team** through **coaching**. Facilitation is designed to overcome the difficulties inherent in a team operating environment. Among the challenges facilitation should resolve are artificial **consensus**, "group think," intermember conflict, and the tendency to become so enamored with the team **process** that the end **objectives** not only aren't reached, but are completely forgotten.

facilitator A **team member** or outside resource who possesses good group process skills and guides the team through **coaching**. Facilitators should have excellent interpersonal skills, be able to synthesize groups of ideas into understandable concepts and effectively communicate them, be prepared to deal effectively with strong and emotional team members while remaining objective, and keep focused on the team's processes for achieving its mission. See also **communication**.

facilitator qualifications The qualifications of a **facilitator** include:

1. The ability to help others reach conclusions and achieve **consensus**.
2. The ability to withstand strong emotional pressures such as bullying, shouting, and crying.
3. The ability to separate himself or herself from the **team** and its **objectives** on an emotional level—that is, detachment and objectivity.
4. The ability to remain focused on the team **problem-solving** process and not get caught up in the problem itself. The facilitator must be able to lead the team through the problem-solving and consensus-building **process** whether he or she believes in the solution the group develops or not.

facilitator's responsibilities See **facilitator's role**.

facilitator's role   The responsibilities of the **facilitator**:

1. Helps the team to clarify the mission
2. Builds the foundation for effective team **communication**
3. Is the neutral guide of the team
4. Does not evaluate or contribute unqualified ideas (unless agreed to in advance by the team)
5. Suggests alternative methods and procedures
6. Protects individuals and their ideas from attack
7. Encourages participation by all on the team
8. Helps the team to come up with win/win solutions
9. Helps to create an atmosphere of synergy within the team
10. Makes certain that outside influences are minimal
11. Works for **consensus** on those items requiring it
12. Focuses on the process of achieving the team's mission
13. Works with the team **leader** to discuss meeting agendas and outcomes

factorial analysis   An analysis procedure in complex **experimental designs**. In factorial analysis, the influence of the experimental factors is evaluated in terms of what their main effect or, in combination with other factors, what their interaction effects have on some criterion measure or quality characteristic (**satisfier**). The designs in which factorial analysis is appropriate may be *full* factorial designs, when each factor level of each factor appears in combination with each and every level of every other factor in the design. Or, since this setup can lead to numerous combinations in complex designs, a *fractional* factorial design may be employed. In both cases, factorial analysis, typically employing **analysis of variance** techniques, is proper and desirable.

failure   In **reliability**, the inability of the equipment to satisfy performance or meet design **specifications** after the equipment has experienced successful operation, or when there is an expectation that the equipment will perform successfully without adjustment/rework. Failure is not confined to mechanical breakage or electrical malfunction. Other forms of failure include the following:

1. Loss of speed
2. Performance degradation
3. Out-of-adjustment conditions

4. Lack of **quality**
5. Leaks
6. Operational malfunction

See also **reliability**.

failure costs See **internal failure costs** and **external failure costs**.

failure mode analysis (FMA) An analysis procedure used for the identification of potential ways in which a system, **process**, or piece of equipment can fail. Once the modes of failure are identified, preventive plans, actions, and options may be developed and implemented to lessen the likelihood that the potential failure modes will become realities. FMA is a component of **reliability** and **advanced quality planning**.

failure mode effects analysis (FMEA) An extension of **failure mode analysis** in which effects of failure are identified (anticipated) as is the mode or method by which failure might occur. Once each failure mode and the effects of such a failure are identified, they are rated according to severity, likelihood of occurrence, and likelihood of being detected. They are then prioritized for preventive action and **control**.

failure mode effects and criticality analysis (FMECA) A technique performed following a **failure mode effects analysis** in which each potential **failure** effect is classified according to its severity and probability of occurrence.

fault tree analysis (FTA) An analysis technique designed to help avoid problems or eliminate historical problems through identification and resolution of **root causes**. The fundamental steps involved in a fault tree analysis are:

1. Identify and clearly define the fault to be addressed.
2. Identify all potential causes of the fault.
3. Define underlying causes for each of the potential causes identified in step 2. Repeat the process at lower and lower levels until root causes are identified.

Standard symbols are used in conducting an FTA to identify the various events and logical associations. See Figure 22.

feedback, customer Information gathered from **customers** as a result of listening to their responses (both positive and negative, both direct and indirect) about the product or service. This feedback occurs in all three stages of the product/service to customer relationship: presale, after sale, and after the product or service's useful life is over. The **objective** of constantly gathering customer feedback is to become and remain consistently aware of **customer needs** and how well they are being met. Formal customer feedback systems take many forms, from simple customer reply cards packaged with the product to full-blown surveys and complex computer systems. Note that customer feedback should be two-way, including feedback to the customer of the work the company is doing on critical customer **satisfiers**. See also **survey-feedback process**.

Feigenbaum, Armand A contemporary **quality** leader who is credited with having invented **total quality control**. Feigenbaum emphasizes quality as a business strategy and a primary source of competitive strength.

Figure 22. **Fault tree symbols.**

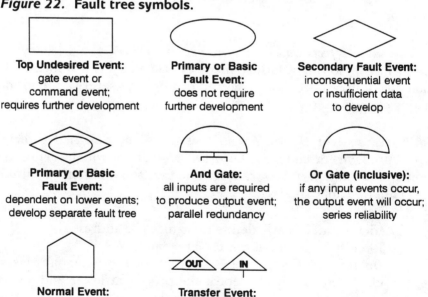

Top Undesired Event:
gate event or
command event;
requires further development

**Primary or Basic
Fault Event:**
does not require
further development

Secondary Fault Event:
inconsequential event
or insufficient data
to develop

**Primary or Basic
Fault Event:**
dependent on lower events;
develop separate fault tree

And Gate:
all inputs are required
to produce output event;
parallel redundancy

Or Gate (inclusive):
if any input events occur,
the output event will occur;
series reliability

Normal Event:
event that must occur

Transfer Event:
information in or out

fishbone diagram or model See **cause-and-effect diagram** and **dispersion analysis**.

fitness for use The degree to which a product or service satisfies the purposes of the **customer**. It is judged by the customer, not by the manufacturer or service provider, and is universally applicable to all goods and services. Parameters for fitness for use include **design quality**, **conformance quality**, and **reliability**. Fitness for use is the **objective** of a three-part system developed by **Juran,** comprised of:

1. *Breakthrough projects.* Includes the creation of a climate for **change**, identification of the **vital few** projects, analysis, overcoming resistance to change, instituting change, and instituting change **controls**. (See also **resistance, planning for**.)

2. *Control sequence.* Includes optimizing the **cost of quality**, establishing the needed professional staff, establishing feedback loops, and establishing a repeated action cycle.

3. *Annual quality program.* Includes establishing quality **objectives** and maintaining the initiative and momentum.

five S's Five Japanese terms perceived by many to represent the fundamental elements of a **total quality management** approach:

1. *Seiri* (organization)
2. *Seiton* (neatness)
3. *Seiso* (cleaning)
4. *Seiketsu* (**standardization**)
5. *Shitsuke* (discipline)

flex-time An approach to employment that includes allowing employees to vary their starting and quitting time each day to suit the needs of their job (fluctuating work load) and their personal needs. Usually, there are **parameters** involved in this type of arrangement such as "Employees may begin their workday any time between 5 A.M. and 9 A.M., and may leave any time between 1 P.M. and 6 P.M."

flexible manufacturing A manufacturing environment typified by factory floor layouts organized by product family. The purpose of flexible manufacturing is to optimize the flow of multiple products through any of a number of series of the work centers involved. The flexibility achieved by layouts and work load balancing resulting from this approach often produces shorter manufacturing **cycle times**, lower inventory levels, and shorter setup times than more traditional approaches where equipment is grouped by type (e.g., all the lathes in one place, all the presses in another place). Machine shops are the most common setting for the deployment of flexible manufacturing today. In machine shops, the parts to be run are assigned a specified amount of capacity on each machine. The machine's available capacity and capability information is stored in a computer database, as is the part routing information, and the machining equipment itself is most often numerically controlled. As parts move through the **process**, the computer continually adjusts priorities to ensure adequate capacity on capable machines is available as needed.

flow chart   A chart representing the steps of a **process**. These charts typically use a standard set of symbols to depict different process steps, including subprocesses, decisions, information storage points, and termination points (see Figure 23). The flow chart is one of the **seven basic tools of quality**. See also **block diagram**.

FMA   See **failure mode analysis**.

FMEA   See **failure mode effects analysis**.

FMECA   See **failure mode effects and criticality analysis (FMECA)**.

focal point chart   A fundamental tool developed for the facilitation of **policy deployment**. The focal point chart provides, on a single document, a listing of measurable and timelined **strategic objectives** selected as a result of a strategic analysis and planning process. The milestones, or focal points, are associated with product performance, **quality**, **defects**, delivery, service, and cost factors important to the **customer** that are in need of a breakthrough rather than tactical (**kaizen**) improvement. (See also **breakthrough improvements**.) They are arranged on this focal point chart according to four major categories:

1. *External customer satisfiers*. Requirements or quality **characteristics**.
2. *External customer dissatisfiers*. **Defects**.

Figure 23. **Flow chart symbols.**

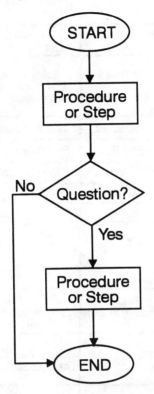

3. *Internal customer needs.* Internally driven business requirements.
4. *Projects.*

The focal point chart serves as the end of the policy deployment
process at each level of the organization. It also serves as the subsequent initiation of the **daily management** function. See Figure 24.
See also **customer needs**, **satisfier**, and **dissatisfier**.

focus factory approach   See **process-oriented flow**.

foolproofing   Fail-safing; a process derived from the Japanese approach called **poka-yoke**. It was initially widely used in machine setups to ensure **accuracy** and vastly reduce the time required to do
the setups. Later, the concept migrated to assembly design, and was

Figure 24. **A focal point chart for the organization of critical characteristics.**

Priority ——— Details	External Customer Needs		Internal Customer Needs	Projects
	Quality Characteristics (Satisfiers)	Defects & Defectives (Dissatisfiers)	Safety, Quality, Operational Costs, Housekeeping, etc.	
1.	Flatness	Scratches	Accident Reduction	New Press Start-Up
2.	Hardness	Edge Burns	Recovery	New Alloy Develop.
3.	Tensile Strength	Voids	Eliminating Cobbles	
4.	Surface Quality	Smears		
5.	Profile			
6.				
How (Strategy)	Quality Improvement Strategy (QIS)	Problem-Solving Strategy (PSS)	Any/All Appropriate Strategy(ies)	Any/All Appropriate Strategy(ies)
Who (Assigned Personnel)	Quality Improvement Team	Problem-Solving Team	Natural Work Teams; Employee Suggestions	Assigned Cross-Functional Project Teams (QIS/PDCA/SDCA)
What (Major Tools)	SPC/SQC Tools; Experimental Design	Deming Wheel; 7 Basic Tools	Any/All Appropriate Tools	Any/All Appropriate Tools

applied in the manner that parts can only be assembled in the intended sequence, with the intended orientation.

force field analysis   A technique used by TQM improvement **teams** to identify the forces at work in an environment. It graphically represents the forces that will support and/or enable the group to reach its desired **objectives**, as well as the forces that impede or restrain progress.

Conducting and using the force field analysis includes the following steps:

1. List the enabling forces and prioritize them in descending order of importance.

2. List the inhibiting or restraining forces on the opposite side of the page in the same manner.
3. Take whatever action is required to eliminate or mitigate the inhibiting forces. (Utilize the **plan-do-check-act** approach.)

fostering innovation   See **innovation, fostering**.

four M's   Terms popularized in conjunction with the **Ishikawa** fishbone diagram, they represent *manpower, methods, materials,* and *machines*. These terms are used to define broad categories of possible problem causes for **problem solving** through identification and elimination of **root causes**. See also **cause-and-effect diagram**.

14 points   Dr. W. Edwards **Deming's** 14 management obligations that are intended to help companies increase their quality and productivity:

1. Create constancy of purpose toward improvement of product and service, with the aim to improve competitive position and to stay in business and provide jobs.
2. Adopt the new philosophy.
3. Cease dependence on inspection to achieve quality.
4. End the practice of awarding business on price alone. Instead, depend on meaningful measures of quality along with price and move toward a single supplier for any one item, on a long-term relationship of loyalty and trust.
5. Improve constantly and forever the system of production and service, to improve quality and productivity, and thus continually decrease cost.
6. Institute training on the job.
7. Adopt and institute leadership.
8. Drive out fear, so that everyone may work effectively for the company.
9. Break down barriers between staff areas and departments.
10. Eliminate slogans, exhortations, and targets for the work force; don't ask for new levels without providing methods to achieve them.
11. Eliminate numerical quotas for the work force and numerical goals for management.
12. Remove barriers that rob people of their right to pride of

workmanship and eliminate the annual rating or merit system.

13. Institute a vigorous program of education and self-improvement for everyone.

14. Put everybody in the company to work to accomplish the transformation; create a system to push every day on the above 13 points.

frequency distribution   A graph that represents the frequency of occurrences for possible outcomes for a data set. Frequency distributions may be ungrouped (each class interval is a single observation) or grouped (outcomes are grouped into class intervals of more than one observation). See also **histogram**.

frequency polygon   A line graph that depicts a **frequency distribution**.

FTA   See **fault tree analysis**.

functional layout   A factory floor layout that groups similar equipment into distinct and separate areas (i.e., all machining equipment in one area, all sheet metal equipment in another area, etc.) This contrasts with the process-oriented layout, which is organized into cells that perform all the production operations for families of parts. Functional layouts typically require more extensive material handling and travel distances and result in more work-in-process inventory than process-oriented layouts. See also **process-oriented flow**, **just-in-time manufacturing**, and **parts flow**.

functional responsibilities   Those duties that are performed as a necessary and value-added part of the daily routine for a specific job function.

funnel experiment   An experiment that illustrates the results of tampering or tweaking. Marbles are placed in a funnel held above a flat-surfaced target. The person conducting the experiment will tend to overcompensate both for missed targets and direct hits, demonstrating that an adjustment made to a stable **process** will often produce worse products than those generated from the process when it is left alone (here, when the funnel is held in one place). See also **tweaking**.

FURSAP measures   A generic set of product attribute categories produced by A. Richard Shores in 1988, which may be used in conjunction with **quality function deployment** to eliminate the confusion common in generating attribute information for QFD **house of quality** activities.

The categories comprising the FURSAP acronym are:

1. Functionability
2. Usability
3. **Reliability** and Performance
4. Supportability/Serviceability
5. Availability
6. Price

G

GAAP   See **generally accepted accounting principles (GAAP)**.

gainsharing   An incentive plan that distributes bonuses on a regular basis to all employees based on the performance of the company. In many companies, the distribution differs in size between levels, but must remain proportionate so that greater company performance equals proportionately greater yield to every employee. In other companies, the distribution is identical for all employees and varies in size only as a direct result of differences in total company performance.

Gantt chart   A chart that uses horizontal bars to depict planned and completed work activities on a scale of time. See Figure 25.

gap analysis   A technique for identifying needed improvements by comparing the current environment and current **processes** against an envisioned future state. After identifying the differences between the two, the

Figure 25. **Gantt chart.**

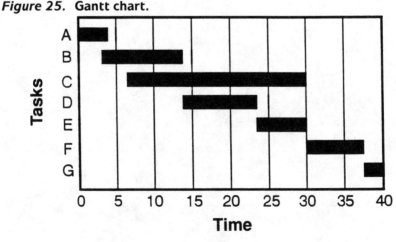

magnitude of the differences between them is analyzed and becomes the basis for defining improvement strategies.

gauge repeatability and reproducibility (studies)   Refers to the analysis of the **precision** of a **measurement process** through the assessment of its:

1. *Repeatability* (σ_{RPT}). The degree to which repeated measures of the same object or specimen yield the same result.
2. *Reproducibility* (σ_{RPD}). The degree to which the means of two or more measurement error **distributions** agree, or **conformance** to the same value.

Note that **measurement error** (σ_E) is a combination of **variability** due to repeatability and reproducibility.

Some **repeatability** and **reproducibility** studies are called R&R studies and are generally conducted at one point in time. These studies may also be conducted over the short and long term; however, in these cases, the assessment of statistical **control** is required. All precision analyses assessing repeatability and reproducibility are used with **continuous data**. Measurement processes associated with **discrete data** for analogous applications are assessed for their reliability, based on internal consistency and concordance.

generally accepted accounting principles (GAAP)   Formal written principles that govern the behavior of certified public accountants, who prepare financial statements, provide tax services, and offer accounting advice and legal opinions about the **accuracy** of a company's financial statements.

generic routings   Manufacturing **process** routings that pertain to a group or family of parts. These routings often depict the physical movement of part families through **cellular manufacturing** operations.

George M. Low Award   See **NASA Award**.

go/no go   A term used to refer to the acceptability of a unit or product. This term reduces all possible conditions to a binary decision about product acceptability: *go* means acceptable (conforms to specification), and *no go* means unacceptable.

goals Defined conditions to be achieved by specific effort applied over the long term. In common terms, a goal is what one sets out to achieve.

goals, strategic Defined conditions that flow from the vision of the organization and that, if achieved, would necessarily result in the attainment of the vision. Strategic goals typically span more than five years in their achievement, and are each further defined as contributory **strategic objectives**.

government/industry partnership A movement away from the adversarial "police officer" role for government versus the "manipulator" role for business, toward a relationship of collaboration toward common **objectives**. This relationship will mean an increased sense of **ownership** for both groups. Government will need to become a better coordinator and **facilitator** of business relationships and infrastructure, and business will need to become a better **customer** for government support through defining its needs in a way that is beneficial to society and useful for government infrastructure designers. In this way, legislation and funding may be directed into channels that promote growth and **stability** for business and the national community with minimal government intervention.

group process techniques A general set of group behavior process guidelines including **problem solving**, **consensus** building, **brainstorming**, and **nominal group technique**.

group technology An approach to design and/or manufacturing that uses the common **characteristics** of parts to gain efficiencies in the utilization of manufacturing resources (such as machine setups) and procurement leverage with suppliers by offering the ability to negotiate prices for entire **commodities** (families) of parts.

growth rate analysis A technique for identifying the rate of growth in a specific technology over time. A minimum of three points are used to identify differences along the growth line of the technology, generally based on the published market size of that technology.

H

Hawthorne effect   A term referring to experiments conducted by Bell Laboratories in the 1920s, which demonstrated that mere management interest in employees and their working conditions affects the productivity of the employees.

hidden factory   That portion of factory capacity that is not used due to waste or poor **asset utilization** in the areas of **availability**, **duty cycle**, **efficiency**, and **recovery**.

hierarchy of improvement   A diagram that helps illustrate the steps required for **continuous improvement** in business. To move up the hierarchy, an organization must develop an infrastructure to support the various levels of improvement. These levels of improvement can be applied to quality, cost, delivery, safety, environment, and morale. These in turn will lead to improved competitive position and customer satisfaction, and, as in a building, if the lower levels are not solid, the entire structure will be weak. See Figure 26.

Figure 26.   **Hierarchy of improvement.**

histogram   A vertical bar graph summarizing the variation in a data set. The histogram's pictorial nature makes it easier for people to identify patterns that are more difficult to discern in a numeric table. See Figure 27. The histogram is one of the **seven basic tools of quality**. See also **frequency distribution**.

hoshin planning   A planning technique that derives its name from the Japanese term *hoshin kanri,* which means "shining metal" and "pointing direction." This planning method uses relatively short-term, high-impact **goals** to achieve breakthrough improvements in company performance. Companies use **vision statements** to develop their **goals, objectives,** and operating strategies. Periodic **audits** are performed to assess and encourage progress toward achieving the envisioned future state. See also **policy deployment**.

house of quality   A graphic tool used in **quality function deployment** that displays and organizes the "whats" of defined **customer needs** and the "hows" of the manufacturing **process**, generating a clear picture of the relationships between what is done in each process of the manufacturing and how these individual activities relate to the defined customer needs. See Figure 28. See also **matrix diagram**.

Figure 27. **Histogram.**

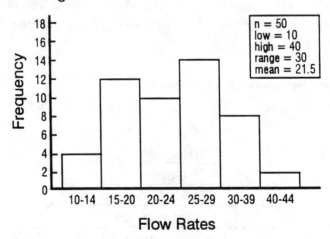

Figure 28. House of quality for making instant coffee with a micro-wave.

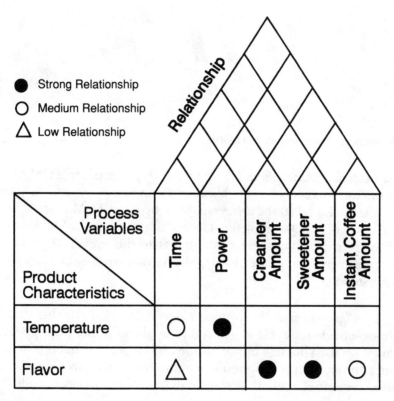

hypothesis An unproven theory, supposition, or assertion that is used to explain certain facts or relationships between variables. Hypotheses are generally used to provide a foundation for further investigation about possible **cause-and-effect** relationships.

I

imperfection   See **nonconformity**.

implementation phase (phase IV)   The fourth phase of the TQM process. (See the Introduction of this publication for an overview of all five phases.) This phase, also called the *deployment phase* by some TQM practitioners, is the portion of a TQM implementation that contains initial pilot activities and long-term management commitment to the overall TQM process. The implementation phase of a TQM program typically involves the following steps:

1. *Alignment with the strategic improvement plan.* In this step, the **plan-do-check-act cycle** is utilized to establish initial pilot programs focused on the **vital few** opportunities and to assure that top management commitment is supplied in a manner that will provide adequate funds, personnel, and other resources to enable success. See also **strategic plan**.

2. *Strengthening the program infrastructure.* In this step, **training** and **team**-building activities are used to support pilot initiatives and to expand the general basis of understanding of TQM principles and concepts.

3. *Initiating the **continuous improvement plan**.* In this step, the organization's **vision** is fully aligned with the planned and ongoing TQM improvement initiatives, such that the organization's future is fully a product of the TQM **continuous improvement** processes. TQM process improvement teams become a way of life in the organization during this step and eventually become integral to the culture of the company. (See also **company culture**.) All improvement team activities are directed toward measurable **objectives** that are aligned with organizational objectives and strategic goals and flow from the company vision and mission. (See also **goals, strategic**.)

4. *Monitoring performance and communicating lessons learned.* In this step, team progress is monitored by executive management, and progress is measured against objective, time-phased milestones. Based on successes and **failures**, three things happen: First, successes are celebrated widely throughout the organization. Second, failures are traced to **root cause** so that **corrective actions** can be documented and these mistakes can be prevented in the next improvement effort. Third, the strategic improvement plan is adjusted and modified as required to incorporate the lessons learned from ongoing initiatives.

importance See **comparative and relative importance**.

important many **Juran's** redefining of the trivial many, a term used in **Pareto analysis**. See also **trivial many**.

improvement, breakthrough See **breakthrough improvement**.

improvement, continuous See **continuous improvement**.

improvement plan See **continuous improvement plan**.

in-control process A process that, when measured statistically, consistently produces only variations that can be attributed to **common causes**. The presence of this situation is generally judged through the use of a **statistical process control** chart. See also **control chart**, **out-of-control process**, **lower control limit**, and **upper control limit**.

in-process inspection **Inspection** of parts within the manufacturing **process**, often performed by the machine operator, using manufacturing tooling as a medium of inspection. This approach contrasts with the off-line inspection that detects **defects** only at widely spaced intervals between manufacturing processes (usually by an autonomous **quality** inspector), allowing more time and inventory to be expended before the condition is detected and remedied. See also **detection**.

in-process testing Testing of manufactured materials, parts, and assemblies during the manufacturing **process**, often by the machine operator. This approach contrasts with the off-line testing traditionally performed at the conclusion of a series of manufacturing operations, where **detection** of the **root cause** is far more difficult and time consuming.

inadvertent error   See **operator-controllable error**.

incursion probability, new technology   A calculation used to estimate the likelihood of new technologies to migrate through any specific area of the manufacturing company. (Refer to *Manufacturing 2000*, W. Duncan, New York: AMACOM, 1994.)

independent variable   Any factor that may have an effect on the **dependent variable** under investigation. Under certain circumstances, the independent variable may also be called a covariate.

individuals chart   See **X chart**.

inference space   A term used to refer to the **population** or universe to which the results of an experiment may be generalized. See also **research population**.

influences, competitor   See **competitor influences**.

information reliability   See **reliability, information**.

information systems architecture   See **architecture, information systems**.

infrastructure management   The identification and manipulation of infrastructure elements. Infrastructure in the business context includes legislative, political, economic, physical, and social foundations for competitive business operations.

innovation Any significant "quantum leap" or breakthrough **change** (especially an improvement) in a method or device. Innovation generally arises from three sources:

   1. *Demand-led innovation,* which results from the desire to overcome labor or material constraints in meeting production demands

   2. *Competitive-led innovation,* which results from market demands for new products and services and the direct pressure of competitors, especially as related to competitive **benchmarking** (see also **competitor influences**)

   3. *Internally generated innovation,* which results from internal research and development, and increasingly from TQM-related improvement activities

innovation, fostering Fostering innovation in a TQM environment is generally a result of using **team**-based **problem solving**. Also, the desire to innovate in order to surpass competitors as experienced in the competitive **benchmarking** process. (See also **competitor influences**.) Especially in manufacturing organizations, **cross-functional teams** have proven very successful in fostering innovations in products as **process** design. And finally, innovations occur most frequently in environments that are nonthreatening, since risk-taking is a part of the nature of innovative activity.

inspecting in quality vs. designing in quality See **detection vs. prevention**.

inspection The measurement of products to compare them against a predefined standard of acceptability. Inspection is generally targeted against a specific set of part characteristics identified as critical to product performance or marketability.

inspection, point-of-use See **point-of-use inspection**.

instant pudding A phrase used to describe the incorrect assumption that **quality** and productivity improvement can be achieved quickly, on faith. The "instant pudding" mindset can be a true obstacle to achieving **quality** as the process requires ample education and effort.

integrated information systems A set of systems so completely integrated that telecommunications, information processing, **electronic data interchange**, and many user interface device **controls** will be virtually indistinguishable from one another.

intelligence, artificial See **artificial intelligence**.

internal customer   See **customer, internal**.

internal failure costs   Components of the **cost of quality** that would disappear if no **defects** existed in the products prior to shipment to the **customer** and if all **specifications** for the product were correct. Examples include scrap, rework, retest, downtime, yield losses, and disposition.

International Standards Organization (ISO)   A worldwide federation of national standards organizations from more than 100 countries. This organization exists to promote international standardization and related activities. Headquartered in Geneva, Switzerland, ISO initiated the **ISO 9000** series of quality standards that have become central to modern TQM activities in a large number of American (and other) businesses.

interval data   Classification according to a continuum, such as ounces or inches. Interval data are characterized by an equality of units and the ability to sensibly divide the units of measure into sub-units (e.g., hours into minutes). See also **continuous data** and **variables data**.

inventory, buffer   See **buffer inventory/stock**.

involvement   See **employee involvement**.

Ishikawa, Kaoru   A quality expert, author, and consultant who has served as president of Kei-dan-ren Federated Economic Societies and the Union of Japanese Scientists and Engineers (JUSE). He developed the Ishikawa diagram (the **cause-and-effect diagram**) and is a recipient of the **Deming Prize.** He also played a key role in introducing **Deming** and Deming's theories to top management in Japan.

Ishikawa diagram   See **cause-and-effect diagram**.

ISO   Acronym for **International Standards Organization**.

ISO 9000   A set of five international standards pertaining to **quality assurance** and **quality** management developed in 1987 and published by the **International Standards Organization.** The standards were developed to harmonize many national and international standards in order to facilitate international and intranational contract establishment and commerce. Because of its breadth, ISO 9000 is necessarily fairly generic and has been criticized in terms of its usefulness. The individual ISO 9000 standards are as follows:

1. *ISO 9000.* Quality Management and Quality Assurance Standards: Guidelines for Selection and Use.
2. *ISO 9001.* Quality Systems—Model for Quality Assurance in Design/Development, Production, Installation, and Servicing.
3. *ISO 9002.* Quality Systems—Model for Quality Assurance in Production and Installation.
4. *ISO 9003.* Quality Systems—Model for Quality Assurance in Final Inspection and Test.
5. *ISO 9004.* Quality Management and Quality System Elements Guidelines.

ISO 9000 registration shows that the company has been **audited** and approved according to the applicable standard(s) by an independent ISO 9000 registrar. See also **certification, ISO 9000.**

isolated peak distribution   In a **distribution** pattern plotted with vertical bars, a small peaked distribution of values that is separate from the larger distribution pattern. This phenomenon usually results from the operation of two or more distinct **processes** in the data **sampled**. See Figure 29.

Figure 29. **Isolated peak distribution.**

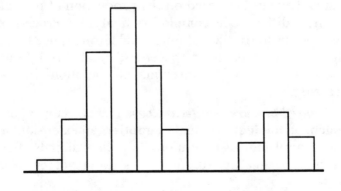

J

JIT   See **just-in-time manufacturing**.

Juran, Joseph M.   One of the first **quality** leaders to deal with the broad management aspects of quality. Juran first introduced the **cost of quality** concept in his book *The Quality Control Handbook* (New York: McGraw-Hill) in 1951. Juran advocates structured improvement initiatives, the sense of urgency, extensive **training**, and strong upper-level management commitment.

JUSE   Union of Japanese Scientists and Engineers.

just-in-time (JIT) manufacturing   A philosophy of **waste** elimination. In a just-in-time environment, the underlying operating principle is that anything that does not add **value** is eliminated or minimized to the greatest possible extent. In manufacturing, all inventory, queue time, and labor that are not required are targeted for reduction. See also **value-added analysis**.

There are several aspects to just-in-time manufacturing, including:

1. *Process-oriented flow.* The **objective** of process-oriented flow is to convert **functional layouts** of machines in the factory into series of **processes**. Layouts are based on the production of product families, or **commodities**. (See **commodity analysis**.) Process-oriented flows are superior to traditional functional layouts since they reduce travel distance, required floor space, and total throughput times. They also lend support to conversion of operations into **cellular manufacturing**.

2. *Advanced procurement technology.* The objective of **advanced procurement technology** is to make **suppliers** an extension of a company's own manufacturing operations. Suppliers directly affect product costs, product **quality**, responsiveness to **customer needs**, and

thereby profitability and viability as a business. In order to maximize the connectivity between a company's operations and those of its suppliers, advanced procurement technology directs that companies move from previously adversarial relationships toward supplier partnerships where contracts are tied to many more aspects of performance than merely price. Quality, delivery performance, and other measures should be included. In addition, supplier capacity may be the object of the contract, rather than merely a specific number of designated parts delivered on a designated date. This cooperative contracting provides for a win/win situation where supplier work **stability** is achieved with maximum production and delivery flexibility for operations. **Electronic data interchange** with suppliers is another important aspect of advanced procurement technology, as are supplier certification programs and involving the supplier in up-front **concurrent engineering** processes.

3. *Improved design methods.* There are two objectives of improved design methods, with one objective related to the design process and the other related to the product designed. Just-in-time techniques may be applied to the process of design engineering to minimize design **work-in-process** and design throughput times. Just-in-time principles should also be applied to the actual design product through applications of concurrent engineering and **value analysis/value engineering** to make the product as efficient and easy to manufacture as possible.

4. *Enhanced support functions.* The objective of enhanced support functions is to use JIT techniques, such as the elimination of non-value-added activity and time to eliminate waste in all support areas. (See **value-added analysis**.)

5. *Employee involvement.* The objective of **employee involvement** in a JIT environment is to use the skills and knowledge of all employees effectively in improvement efforts, and to enhance "buy-in" to improvement initiatives. There are several approaches to employee involvement, such as **quality circles** and employee suggestion programs. See **suggestion systems**.

6. *Enhanced quality.* The enhancement of overall product and process quality levels is an essential element of JIT manufacturing. In a JIT environment, a central objective is to eliminate **defects** since defects are a major cause and result of waste in many resource areas. JIT efforts, therefore, often include initiatives to ensure that designs

will result in quality products, that **process capability** will result in quality products, and so forth. All JIT implementations include a central emphasis on quality, and most TQM programs adopted in manufacturing operations include one or more initiatives that focus on JIT operations.

7. *Simplified, synchronous production.* The objective of simplified, **synchronous production** is to convert individual manufacturing activities into elements of a continuous manufacturing flow synchronized to end-product demand. **Lot sizes** are reduced in this process and materials are "pulled" from operation to operation in manufacturing. (See also **pull system**.)

K

kaizen A Japanese term for continuous improvement, founded on the principles of doing little things better and setting, working toward, and achieving increasingly higher standards. Masaaki Imai, author of the book *Kaizen: The Key to Japan's Competitive Success* (New York: Random House, 1986), states that quality deployment is regarded to be the most significant development to come out of **total quality control** since the mid-1960s. He also emphasizes **policy deployment** as a central aspect to making **quality** pervade the entire organization. See also **continuous improvement** and **breakthrough improvements**.

kanban A Japanese term that is the cornerstone of the just-in-time **pull system**. Kanban actually means "to put away and to bring out." In pull systems, it often refers to a card or other physical device used to signal the previous operation that it is authorized to produce the next unit. See also **synchronous production**.

kurtosis A **shape** parameter (γ_4) that indicates the flatness or "peakedness" of a **distribution**. It is also called "the fourth moment about the **mean**, or γ_4 (population) and g_4 (sample)." Normal (Gaussian) distributions are referred to as *Mesokurtic* in nature; *meso* indicating an intermediate level of peakedness. Distributions that are higher in the peak and lower in the tails than a Mesokurtic distribution are called *Leptokurtic*. Distributions that are lower in the peak and higher in the tails than Mesokurtic functions are called *Platykurtic* distributions. Underlying **population** distributions that are Mesokurtic possess a theoretical γ_4 value of 0.0. Theoretical population functions that are Leptokurtic possess positive γ_4 values. Platykurtic functions reflect negative γ_4 indices. See Figure 30. See also **normal distribution** and **skewness**.

Figure 30. **The general forms of kurtosis.**

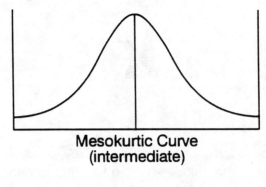

Mesokurtic Curve
(intermediate)

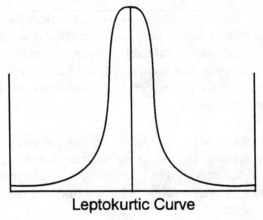

Leptokurtic Curve

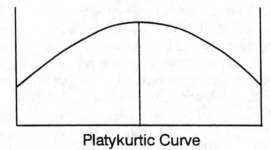

Platykurtic Curve

L

latent defects   **Defects** that are not identified until they are experienced during **customer** ownership. Latent defects are generally caused by inadequate design margin, product complexity, and/or low **process capability**. The solution to latent defects most often lies in increasing the ratio of design margin to process capability.

LCL   See **lower control limit**.

lead team, business   See discussion under **planning phase (phase II)**.

lead time   The time ahead of a specified milestone at which the prior activity must be started. In manufacturing, there are several segments of lead time. For example, **material requirements planning** systems usually contain manufacturing lead time to produce the product, **supplier** lead times (to procure parts for the product), and move and queue times for material handling between production operations. See also **cycle time**.

leader, team   A member of a team with a vested interest in the team's success and one who is willing to help the team stay focused.

leader's role   The responsibilities of the **leader**:

1. Should be content focused
2. Is accountable for outcomes, assignments and record keeping, and progress checks
3. Should work with the team facilitator to discuss meeting outcomes and meeting agenda design (who will do what, etc.)
4. Is a full-fledged **team member**
5. Can serve as the team's coach regarding content
6. Should be the primary contact with the team sponsor

leadership   The ability to create a **vision**, clearly communicate that vision to others, and then motivate those others to achieve the envisioned state. Leadership is an absolutely critical element of any TQM implementation. See also **communication** and **motivation**.

leadership processes   The primary processes performed by top-level management leaders in a TQM environment. According to Svenson et al. in *The Quality Roadmap* (New York: AMACOM, 1994), these processes include strategic planning, operational planning, budget control, **empowerment**, and results measurement.

leptokurtic   See **kurtosis**.

listening to the customer   See **customer mapping process**.

little q   See **big Q, little q**.

LL   See **lower limit**.

logistics, design for   See **design for logistics**.

loss function, Taguchi   See **Taguchi loss function**.

lot   In a TQM context, a quantity of parts to be accumulated for purposes of **sampling**. In the more common manufacturing context, the term *lot* is used to refer to a group of parts or product (often physically in one container) traveling together through the manufacturing **process**.

lot size   The quantity of product or number of units (or parts) within a lot. See **lot**.

Low (George M.) Award   See **NASA Award**.

lower control limit (LCL)   The lower boundary, drawn as a horizontal dashed line on a **control chart**, indicating the value above which sample (statistical) values may fluctuate when the **process** is in a state of **control**. A full and proper assessment of control requires consideration of process performance with respect to the **upper control limit** and laws of probability in addition to the lower control limit. See **control limit** and **in-control process**.

lower limit (LL) A term used by different practitioners to refer (ambiguously) to **lower specification limit, lower process limit,** or **lower control limit.**

lower process limit The threshold below which exactly .135% of the measures, scores, values, or observations fall.

lower specification limit (LSL) The point below which any measured value of a critical characteristic will result in a **defective** product in that it no longer conforms to **specifications**. See also **process capability** and **conformance.**

LSL See **lower specification limit.**

M

machine shop   See **flexible manufacturing**.

Malcolm Baldrige Award   See **Malcolm Baldrige National Quality Award**.

Malcolm Baldrige National Quality Award   An annual award to recognize U.S. companies that excel in quality management and quality achievement. The award was created by Public Law 100–107 in 1987 and supported by the Foundation for the Malcolm Baldrige National Quality Award, established in 1988. The award is named for Malcolm Baldrige, who served as secretary of commerce from 1981 until his tragic death in a rodeo accident in 1987. The award is administered by the **American Society for Quality Control**, under contract to the National Institute of Standards and Technology (NIST). The award has three eligible categories: manufacturing companies, service companies, and small businesses. Up to two awards may be given in each category annually. Companies participating in the award process submit applications that include completion of the award examination application and review by a board of examiners.

MAN   See **metropolitan area network**.

management, daily   See **daily management**.

management by objective (MBO)   An approach to management of performance through the establishment of annual **objectives** for each employee and rating the performance of the employees at the end of the performance period (typically this is an annual process cycle) based on performance to those objectives. Note that this approach is not an element of **total quality management**, but is an "old school" methodology that is in contrast with a quality philosophy. See also **14 points**, especially point 11.

management by policy   See **policy deployment**.

management-controllable error   See **operator self-control**.

management of constraints   See **constraint management**.

manpower, methods, materials, and machines   See **four M's**.

manufacturing resource planning (MRP II)   A software system composed of multiple autonomous and semi-autonomous modules, including part master files, a bill of materials module, **master scheduling**, **material requirements planning**, procurement management, shop floor activity **control**, inventory management, and **distribution requirements planning**. Very large MRP II systems have also grown to encompass previously separate software modules such as accounts payable and accounts receivable, and an engineering database.

manufacturing styles   See **batch manufacturing**, **cellular manufacturing**, and **flexible manufacturing**.

mapping process, customer   See **customer mapping process**.

market share, importance of   The value of this indicator of market position. According to many leading business analysts, market share is an essential measure of company health, and one of the most powerful predictors of the company's future. Buzzell and Gale, in their book *The PIMS Principles* (New York: Free Press, 1987), say:

> The 1960s and 1970s brought a dawning realization that market share is key to a company's growth and profitability. The 1980s have shown just as clearly that one factor above all others—**quality**—drives market share. And when superior quality and large market share are both present, profitability is virtually guaranteed.

master manual   A method of documenting the TQM program in order to lend consistency and structure throughout the different functional areas and **processes** of the organization. The master manual is actually a set of manuals. One manual is kept in each department. Another is kept that summarizes the manuals in all the departments within a division, and so on, up to the overall company master manual. The manual should provide continuity of structure by depicting the flow-down of company **vision** and **mission statements** through policies and practices down to individual operating procedures. It should also provide the linkage between TQM improvement team initiatives and overall company strategy. Finally, the master manual system should provide clear documentation of the company **quality** system, supporting the company's efforts in the areas of **Malcolm Baldrige National Quality Award** application and/ or **ISO 9000** registration. A fairly comprehensive outline of master manual contents and uses is provided in *The TQM Trilogy,* by Mahoney and Thor (New York: AMACOM, 1994).

master scheduling   The overall production schedule that drives the production of the manufacturing organization through the loading of end-product delivery dates (known as *independent demand*) into the **material requirements planning** system. The **accuracy** of the master production schedule is essential to effective manufacturing materials planning.

material flow   See **parts flow**.

material handling, automated   See **automated material handling**.

material requirements planning (MRP)   A computerized system of planning the purchase and/or production of parts from raw material through end-item delivery. The MRP system uses a structured bill of material for the product, and applies **lead time** offsets to determine when each component must be procured or fabricated in order to support assembly and delivery of the finished product. MRP also offers the option to apply any of a number of lot sizing alternatives and general inventory policies (such as reorder points, safety stock levels, and scrap factors) to material and production planning activities. MRP is generally offered by software suppliers as one module of a complete software system called **manufacturing resource planning**, which is much broader in scope.

materials, designer   See **designer materials**.

matrix, decision   See **decision matrix**.

matrix diagram   The central portion of a **quality function deployment house of quality** diagram. This matrix compares the needs of the **customer** to the activities performed within the company. The relationships between activities performed and **customer needs** are identified as weak, medium, or strong in order to target improvement efforts.

MBO   See **management by objective**.

mean   An arithmetic average. In a statistical context, the mean refers to the **central tendency** of a **distribution**, around which the scores or values of a **sample** set are distributed. See also **arithmetic mean**.

mean sums of squares   The value calculated by dividing the sum of squares from the target factor by its **degrees of freedom**. The result is an unbiased estimate of the **variability** of a factor in a given **population**.

mean time between failures (MTBF)   The average time between a repairable product's failures for a specific unit of measure (e.g., operating hours or cycles).

mean time to first failure (MTTFF)   The average time interval between the first usage of a repairable product and the first failure of that product for a defined unit of measure (e.g., operating hours or miles).

mean time to repair (MTTR)   The average length of time required to restore the machine or system to an operable state after it has become inoperable and repairs have been initiated.

means, analysis of   See **analysis of means**.

measurement, evolution of business   A look at business measures over time. Traditionally, business measures were all financially based and offered only a historical view of business performance within a fairly narrow frame of reference. In the 1990s, however, business measures have become broader in order to become more predictive of future performance and more relevant in terms of the competitive position of the company within its industry. Business measures are becoming higher-level metrics with more comprehensive scope, such as market share. (See **market share, importance of**.) In addition, measures are growing more tightly linked from top to bottom throughout the company and focusing increasingly on **process**-oriented measurement criteria.

measurement error   The difference between measured values and actual values for the dimension measured. See also **true value**.

measurement process   The combination of equipment (instruments, gauges, fixtures, etc.), standards, procedures, operators, and environmental **characteristics** operating on an input (product or **process** to be measured) and producing an output (measurement).

median   The middle of a set of data points, or the point that separates the data into halves. Fifty percent of the data values fall below the median, and 50% fall above it. The median is also referred to as the separation **boundary** between the second and third quartile of data.

median and range ($\overline{X} - R$) chart   A **control chart** that uses the **median** and the range of sample values recorded in order to determine whether a **process** is in **control** or if an assignable cause is present and should be addressed. See **in-control process**.

mesokurtic   See **kurtosis**.

metric   See **tactical metrics**.

metropolitan area network (MAN)   A computer and telecommunications network that connects the individual local area networks (LANs) into a larger interactive network.

middle management's role in TQM   A look at the part middle management plays in TQM implementation. The role of middle management in a TQM environment is to communicate and consistently/ effectively manage the conversion of executive-level strategies through TQM improvement initiatives. This linkage is often missing in failed and failing TQM programs. Middle management is responsible for chartering the specific improvement initiatives, monitoring **team**-level progress, communicating successes and challenges to the executive level, securing required resource deployment from executive levels, and sharing "best practices" developed by individual improvement **teams** with the entire company. See also **communication** and **chartering a team**.

mission statement   A statement based on the **vision**, the guiding values and principles of the company. The mission statement is a fundamental element of **policy deployment**. (See also **organizational values**.) Among the components listed in an effectively constructed mission statement are the organization's:

1. *Business* (what the organization does)
2. *Customers* (who the organization's **customers** are)
3. *Plans for the future* (where the organization is going over the coming decade)

mode   The score or value that occurs most frequently in a set of observations.

motivation   The reasons why people take certain action. In a TQM environment, the foundation for motivated employees is put into place with effective development and deployment of the **vision** and strategies. Once this foundation is in place, motivation becomes a function of **communication**, reward systems, individual **empowerment**, and the charisma of the **leadership** involved. See also **reward and recognition system**.

moving range chart   See **R$_M$ chart**.

MR chart   Moving range chart. See **R$_M$ chart**.

MRP   See **material requirements planning**.

MRP II   See **manufacturing resource planning**.

MTBF   See **mean time between failures**.

MTTFF   See **mean time to first failure**.

MTTR   See **mean time to repair**.

mu (μ)   The **mean** of a **population** or universe.

multivariate charts   A type of chart that depicts multiple types of variation simultaneously. (For example, multivariate charts may depict the level of variation over time and also the level of variation from piece to piece.) This chart helps the user take a good preliminary step in narrowing the field of potential causes of variation for designing an experiment.

N

N   The size of a finite **population** or **lot**.

n   The number of units represented in a **sample** (**sample size**).

NASA Award   The National Aeronautics and Space Administration (NASA) Quality and Excellence Award. This award was created in 1985 to heighten the importance of **quality** for NASA's contractors. It was recently renamed the George M. Low Award, in honor of a former NASA deputy administrator. This award is usually given in two categories: large business and small business. The categories covered include performance achievements (including such areas as cost, schedule, and quality) and process achievements (including such areas as commitment, **communication**, planning, **training**, and awards/recognition.)

National Institute of Standards and Technology (NIST)   A group within the U.S. Department of Commerce that distributes copies of the Malcolm Baldrige guidelines to the public and governs the **Malcolm Baldrige National Quality Award**. The address is:

> National Institute of Standards and Technology
> Route 270 and Quince Orchard Road
> Administration Building, Room A537
> Gaithersburg, MD 20899

natural language processors   See **artificial intelligence**.

natural tolerance   The range corresponding to **upper process limit–lower process limit** for a process or population **distribution** within which the middle 99.73% of the scores will fall.

natural work group   A group of people that share a common work area and regularly spend most of their working time together.

natural work team   A **natural work group** that has a clearly defined mission, usually **continuous improvement**.

NDE   See **nondestructive evaluation**.

NDT   See **nondestructive testing**.

needs, customer   See **customer needs**.

networking phase (phase V)   The final phase of the TQM process. (See the Introduction of this publication for an overview of all five phases.) In this phase, the successes of the internal TQM process improvements are fully exploited and outside organizations (especially suppliers) are brought into the improvement activity. The networking (or diversification) phase is comprised of five steps:

1. *The strategic improvement plan is communicated with outside organizations.* The two most important outside entities with whom this information should be shared are **customers** and **suppliers**. It's important to share the information with customers to ensure that what the company is planning will achieve the ultimate **goal** of satisfying **customer needs**. It's critical to share the plan with suppliers, especially key suppliers, in order to bring their improvement plans into alignment and generate opportunities for shared savings from these improvement activities.

2. *"Lessons learned" and current examples of TQM operational successes should be shared with these outside organizations.* This step bolsters customer confidence and promotes brand loyalty. It also demonstrates clearly to suppliers that what you are asking them to do really does work and that you have proven this in a "live" work environment.

3. *Customers and suppliers should be visited on a regular basis.* Strong linkages from the customer through the supplier must be developed to improve responsiveness along the **value**-adding chain and to anticipate the customers' needs.

4. *The TQM process must be institutionalized.* This step involves making the TQM process into the formal operating process of the company through adopting the necessary changes in policies, procedures, standard practices, purchase contracts, customer requirements documentation, and so on.

5. *The process must be developed into a continuous loop.* In other words, the process is repeated over and over again, institutionalizing **continuous improvement**. This will require the constant resetting of goals, continuous learning on the part of everyone in the organization, and continuous **benchmarking** activity.

NIST See **National Institute of Standards and Technology**.

nominal data Discrete data with only two classifications. For example, numeric values that represent open circuit vs. closed circuit, usable vs. unusable, and occurs vs. does not occur. The **control charts** used for nominal data are the **np-chart** and the **c-chart**.

nominal group technique A technique generally used by problem-solving **teams** following **brainstorming** activity. This approach uses ideas jotted down silently and independently on slips of paper, after which the ideas are read off by each individual, and the group prioritizes the ideas to reach **consensus** on the approach to be taken.

nominal value The **customer**-defined or related optimum condition as measured for a critical quality **characteristic**. See also **target value**.

nonconformity The **failure** of a product or service to fulfill a specified requirement. Also, the presence of an attribute or **characteristic** that, due to count, frequency, or both, is found objectionable by the **customer** or consumer. See also **defect**.

nondestructive evaluation (NDE) The evaluation of a product that does not negatively affect the serviceability of the product.

nondestructive testing (NDT) The testing of a product that does not negatively affect the usability or serviceability of the product. In statistical analysis, a nondestructive test is one where the **true value** associated with the specimen evaluated is reobtainable; that is, it does not change as a result of time, testing, or both. See also **destructive testing**.

normal distribution A symmetric, unimodal, bell-shaped **distribution** of continuous data where **skewness** (γ_3) and **kurtosis** (γ_4) both equal zero. See Figure 31. See also **bell-shaped curve**.

Figure 31. **Normal distribution.**

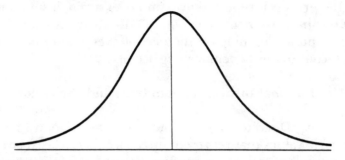

np-chart   A **control chart**, based on the approximation of the **bino-mial distribution**, depicting the number of **defective** units per **sam-ple** over time (used when the sample size remains constant from sam-ple to sample).

O

objective   Statement of a specific result that is to be accomplished within a designated period of time.

OC curve   See **operating characteristic curve**.

ODA/ODIF   See **office document architecture/office document interchange format**.

office document architecture/office document interchange format (ODA/ODIF)   An information technology standard for office document formats that is in the early stages of acceptance in U.S. markets. It is expected that, with International Standards Organization backing, ODA will gain widespread support in Europe before it attains a significant level of acceptance within the United States.

open systems interconnection (OSI)   A standard that will be followed by suppliers who offer **integrated information systems** throughout the second half of the 1990s. More formally known as the International Standards Organization (ISO) Open Systems Interconnection model.

operating characteristic (OC) curve   A graph useful in many areas of **quality** and statistics and also in other areas. In this graph, the vertical axis represents the probability of an event occurring or of taking some action (such as accepting a shipment or rejecting a hypothesis). The horizontal axis represents the magnitude or amount of a characteristic or property upon which the occurrence of the event (or the decision) is based. In quality activities, OC curves are commonly used to indicate the changing probability of accepting a **lot** or a shipment under increasing "true" **defect** rate contamination of the lot. OC curves are also used commonly in statistics to describe the probability of observing a particular statistical value (such as a given mean difference) under increasing amounts of "true" population mean difference (also called **effect size**). Because the probabilities represented on OC curves are frequently dependent on sample size and effect size, they are helpful in determining the proper sample size for different kinds of investigations.

operating plan   See **business plan**.

operation control feedback   The feedback resulting from mechanisms developed to measure the success of improvement initiatives in overall operations performance. This feedback provides clear evidence of the level of improvement or degradation in operations, and when effectively developed, links the visible changes to specific TQM initiatives underway in the business. Feedback should include the information that is deemed to be critical and necessary to monitor/manage the improvement efforts. It should be formatted in a clear and structured manner that is sensible and useful to the management audience. It should also include thresholds defining when **corrective action** will occur.

The primary source of operation control feedback is **process**-level metrics (the metrics developed to reflect the performance of the individual processes of the business). Secondary sources of operation control feedback include **suggestion systems**, **quality** surveys, and **audits** (such as Baldrige criteria audits and **ISO 9000** criteria audits).

operational definition   The definition of terms, variables, constructs, or concepts by the means or methods used to measure or manipulate them. The purpose of an operational definition is to allow one to bring the term, variable, construct, or concept into quantitative empirical reality. Therefore, it is important to make explicit and public the specific steps and actions taken to measure, assess, or manipulate an event or phenomenon of interest. This is accomplished by the operational definition. As an example, one could operationally define general employee satisfaction in terms of the number of days each employee is absent from work, whereas another could define employee satisfaction in terms of the score of an employee satisfaction survey. The strength of a given material might be operationally defined as the force, in pounds, required to break it; another could define it in terms of its resistance to penetration; and yet another could define it in terms of hours of use in a particular application before failure.

operator-controllable error   Error that operators can monitor, detect, and work to prevent. (See also **detection vs. prevention**.) **Standard operating**

procedures (SOPs) and standardization efforts need to be designed to minimize operator-controllable error. In effect, we must plan to reduce human error with our SOPs.

There are three types of operator-controllable errors: inadvertent, technique, and conscious.

1. *Inadvertent errors*, which must be planned for in the creation of SOPs and work methods. Inadvertent errors are the result of the natural incapacity for humans to pay attention 100% of the time. Distinguishing features of inadvertent errors are:

   A. *Unintentional*. The operator does not want to make the error.

   B. *Unwitting*. At the point of making the error, the operator has no knowledge that he or she has just made an error.

   C. *Unpredictable*. No one knows beforehand just when a worker will make an error, or the type of error that will be made. Also, no one knows who will be the next operator to make an error.

2. *Technique errors*, which arise because the operator lacks some essential technique, knowledge, or skill needed to avoid making the error. Distinguishing features of technique errors include:

   A. *Unintentional*. The operator wants to do good work.

   B. *Selective*. The errors are confined to those error categories for which the missing technique is essential.

   C. *Consistent*. Operators possessing the technique can consistently avoid making the errors and the operators who lack the technique will consistently make the error.

   D. *Witting and unwitting*. Technique errors can be of both kinds. Operators may realize at the time that they have just committed an error, but they lack the technique to prevent it from happening (e.g., a golfer who knows when he or she is consistently slicing the ball). The opposite is also true in that an operator may not realize that his or her lack of technique may result in premature product failure or waste further downstream or at the customer site.

   E. *Unavoidable by the unaided operator*. Operators lacking the technique do not know what should be done differently from the current procedure. Therefore, the error can go on and on without some assistance to eliminate it.

The evidence of technique errors is the presence of a consistent difference in error rates among workers. These consistent differences in error rates are selective to specific error types. Within technique errors, there are two subcategories of errors:

        A. *Best practice.* This occurs when a minority of operators possess the technique, knowledge, or skill that is essential to avoid making the error.

        B. *Damaging practice.* This occurs when a minority of operators lack the technique, knowledge, or skill that is essential to avoid making the error.

    3. *Conscious errors*, which operators know they are making and usually intend to keep making.

    Distinguishing features of conscious errors include:

        A. *Intentional.* The error is the result of a deliberate intention by the operator to commit the error.

        B. *Witting.* At the time the error is made, the operator knows that an error has been made.

        C. *Consistent.* The operators who cause conscious errors usually do so on a continuing basis.

operator self-control   The knowledge and action to meet all **quality**, safety, and productivity standards. To reach such a state, the operators must be supplied with the following:

    1. *The means of knowing what is expected of them.* What are they supposed to do? This knowledge can come in the form of **training**, **specifications**, samples of good and bad product, **standard operating procedures**, instructions, etc. It is important, though, that this knowledge is clear and unequivocal.

    2. *The means of knowing what their actual performance is.* Are they doing what they should do? This knowledge can come in the form of **control charts**, **process** measurements, **inspections**, information from **daily management boards**, feedback from downstream processes, and information from the **customer** feedback system, etc. What is important here is that operators know whether or not they are meeting their assigned responsibilities. (See also **feedback, customer.**)

    3. *The means for regulation.* If the actual performance does not meet the desired performance, how will the operators change what

they are doing? Regulation can come in the form of **reaction plans**, product disposition plans, and process adjustment procedures, etc.

If all these needs and criteria have been met, without exception, then the operators are in a state of self-control. They have all the means needed to do good work and any errors are operator-controllable. (See **operator-controllable errors**.) If any of these criteria or needs have not been met, then the managerial job has not been completed. Therefore, all resulting errors are considered management-controllable.

ordinal data Quantitative data that provide a classification according to order. The magnitude of the ordered values may not, however, represent uniform differences. Ordinal data generally are one of three types:

1. *Count data,* such as number of scratches or number of inclusions.
2. *Subjective scale data (also called rank data),* derived from responses to an evaluative scale. For example:

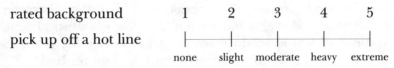

3. *Low-resolution data,* commonly obtained from measuring a continuous underlying function with a gauge or device having limited measurement **resolution**.

The **control charts** used for ordinal data are the **c-chart** and the **u-chart**. See also **attribute data**.

organizational structure and levels The three conceptual levels of organizational structure that have distinct and separate roles in a TQM implementation:

1. *Upper-level or executive management.* Sets strategy, monitors progress, and manages improvement efforts at the highest level. (See also **executive's role in TQM**.)
2. *Middle management.* Defines and develops improvement proj-

ects around the **processes** of the company. (See also **middle management's role in TQM**.)
3. *Working level* (**teams** and individuals). Focuses on implementation of the improvement initiatives.

organizational values The principles that create an organization's culture. (See **company culture**.) These are often most clearly evidenced in general operating characteristics such as internal competition vs. internal teamwork; emphasis on protecting proprietary data vs. open relationships with **customers** and **suppliers**; **continuous improvement** vs. "if it ain't broke, don't fix it." Often, in environments where TQM implementations are not successful, one strongly contributing reason is that the working values of the company are different from the ones formally stated in company literature and by the company's executive leaders. Since one of the most powerful influences on company culture is the example set by upper-level management, this problem can only be remedied when company executives begin to demonstrate a personal commitment to TQM principles in their daily business activities.

OSI See **open systems interconnection**.

out-of-control process A **process** in which the **characteristic**(s) under statistical evaluation are not in a state of statistical **control** due to the effects of **special causes** of variation. See Figure 32. See also **in-control process**, **lower control limit**, and **upper limit**.

out-of-spec, out-of-specification Terms indicating that a unit(s) does not meet **conformance** requirements. See also **specification**.

overall equipment effectiveness See **asset utilization**.

ownership Having the legitimate power and authority to carry out a designated action item. It is important to note that under some circumstances legitimate ownership may exist without the ownership actually being accepted by the individual involved. Another situation can arise when individuals assume ownership without any legitimate power or authority. The bottom line in real terms is that when a person or group assumes responsibility for the performance of a **process**, and has the ability to effect change in that process (whether that power is legitimate or not), there is ownership. This concept is very important. Many times, TQM implementations are ruined by

Figure 32. Patterns indicating possible out-of-control conditions.

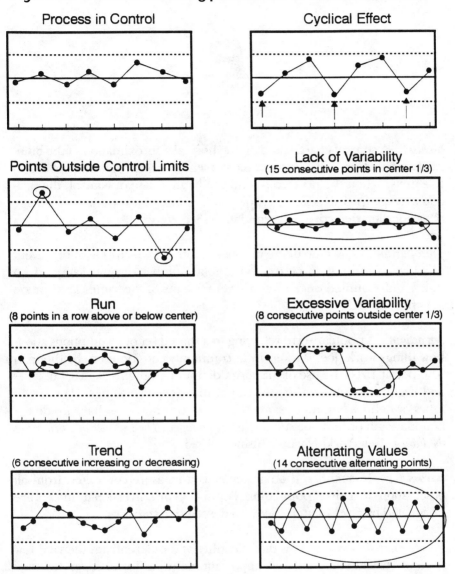

appointing individuals or **teams** to improve a process when the team or individual has no interest and refuses to become actively involved. In these situations, the ownership is official, but inconsequential. As a result, no improvement occurs and usually TQM is blamed for the **failure**. See also **employee involvement**.

P

p-chart   A **control chart**, based on the normal approximation of the **binomial distribution**, reflecting sample percentages or proportions of **defective** units. When the **process** is found to be in a state of **control**, the process average (p-BAR) can be employed to estimate π (pi), the percentage or proportion **defective** in a **population**. See Figure 33.

p-proportion   The ratio of the number of units in which at least one event of a given classification occurs to the total number of units **sampled**. (A unit is only counted once even if several events of the same classification are encountered.)

paradigm   A popular term referring to a shared set of assumptions about how things work. Joel Barker, most commonly considered to be the man who popularized the use of this term, defines paradigms as "a set of rules and regulations (written or unwritten) that does two things: (1) it establishes or defines **boundaries**; and (2) it tells you how to behave inside the boundaries in order to be successful." (*Paradigms, The Business of Discovering the Future,* New York: Harper Business, 1993.)

parameter   In statistics, the parameter is a measure computed from all observations in a given **population**. Population or universe parameters are designated by Greek letters. See also **descriptive statistics**.

Pareto analysis   An analysis that identifies and differentiates the **vital few** from the **trivial many** (or the "important many" as **Juran** suggested they may in fact be). Pareto analysis was originally developed by Vilfredo Pareto, a nineteenth-century Italian economist who discovered this relationship in the context of wealth and its distribution among the general population. The principle was defined in its broader context by **Juran** in 1950. In almost any population, 20% of the population represent 80% of the value in that population. When ranked in descending order, it becomes

Figure 33. **Percent chart (p-chart).**

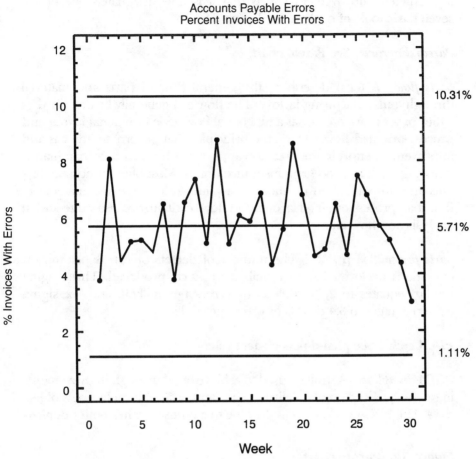

Accounts Payable Errors
Percent Invoices With Errors

relatively easy to identify the most significant items to **control**. For example, when performing cycle counts of inventory, the highest dollar value items should be counted most frequently. In most cases, this means that counting just 20% of the part numbers involved will cover 80% of the dollars in inventory. Similarly, when identifying where to focus improvement efforts, a Pareto analysis is often used to identify the relatively few causes that generate most of the problem conditions.

Pareto chart   A graph (usually a bar chart) that depicts the values of charted occurrences in descending order, identifying those that represent roughly 20% of the occurrences and roughly 80% of the value of the occurrences measured. The ranking of **defect** causes from most to least significant in this manner has become such a popular approach to focusing targeted improvement efforts that it is now designated one of the **seven basic tools of quality**. See Figure 34.

Pareto diagram   See **Pareto chart**.

parts flow   A term describing the general flow of parts and material through a manufacturing factory. The flow can generally be described as either **process** oriented or as a functional flow. (See **functional layout** and **process-oriented flow**.) The same principles that govern an analysis and improvement effort in this area also apply to businesses other than manufacturing, such as processing insurance claims. Most often, functional layouts and flows result in far more non-value-added time and material in flow than process-oriented layouts and flows contain. See also **value-added analysis** and **flow charts**.

parts per million (PPM)   The number of **defects** or errors per million operations performed or per million products produced. Three sigma ($\pm\ 3\sigma$) equates to 2,700 defects or errors per million, and **six sigma** ($\pm\ 6\sigma$) equates to 3.4 defects or errors per million.

PDCA cycle   See **plan-do-check-act cycle**.

PDCA discipline   A strategy used to achieve **breakthrough improvements** in safety, **quality**, morale, delivery, cost, and other critical business **objectives**. The PDCA philosophy is the glue that binds together **policy deploy-**

Figure 34. **Pareto chart.**

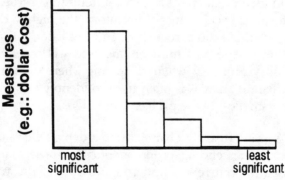

Categories (e.g., defect types)

ment and **daily management** into a cohesive set of **processes**. Break-through improvements are best achieved and sustained by individuals and **teams** using the scientific method as it is expressed in the **plan-do-check-act cycle** broken down into easily implemented steps. See Figure 35. See also **total quality management**.

PDCA management discipline Fosters the use of the **plan-do-check-act cycle** in the implementation of **continuous improvement, standardization,** and **innovation** structure so that planning and feedback become an integral part of management systems and procedures. See Figure 36.

PDCA strategy See **PDCA discipline**.

percent chart See **p-chart**.

Figure 35. The plan-do-check-act discipline within policy deployment.

Figure 36. Evolution of the PDCA management discipline and modern management PDCA cycle.

P	1. Determine goals and targets.
	2. Determine methods of reaching goals.
D	3. Engage in education and training.
	4. Implement work.
C	5. Check the effects of implementation.
A	6. Take appropriate action.

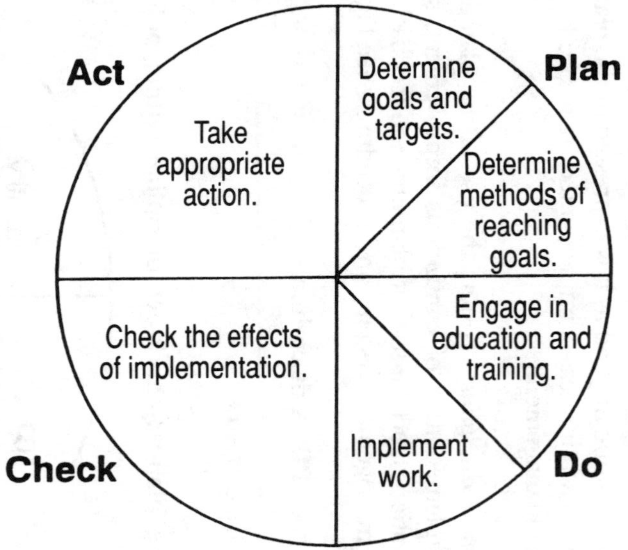

Adapted from Ishikawa.

perceptual map   See **customer map**.

PERT   See **program evaluation and review technique**.

PERT chart   A chart produced by the PERT (program evaluation and review technique) process that reflects the sequential interdependencies in major activities. PERT charts, also called **arrow diagrams**, are often used to manage large projects.

phase I, preparation phase   See **preparation phase (phase I)**.

phase II, planning phase   See **planning phase (phase II)**.

phase III, assessment phase   See **assessment phase (phase III)**.

phase IV, implementation phase   See **implementation phase (phase IV)**.

phase V, networking phase   See **networking phase (phase V)**.

PIT   Process improvement team. See also **planning phase (phase II)**.

plan, business   See **business plan**.

plan-do-check-act (PDCA) cycle   As described in **PDCA management discipline**, this cyclic approach is comprised of four steps: plan, do, check, and act. Though often used in problem solving, as illustrated in the following example, PDCA has other applications (e.g., in a project to implement new software):

1. *Plan*. After one or more factors are identified as causal to a **process** problem, possible solutions are **brainstormed** and the most attractive solution approach is selected. Then the implementation is planned.

2. *Do*. The solution is implemented. This is usually done in a pilot setting as opposed to beginning immediately with the entire population of possible applications, in order to minimize risk while the effectiveness of the solution is proven effective.

3. *Check*. Confirm and document the effects of the action taken. This is frequently accomplished through process **control chart** data

and through before-and-after studies. If the solution proves ineffective, the **team** returns to the plan stage and begins again.

4. *Act.* This involves deploying the solution across the entire population of possible applications, once it has been proven effective, and making it a permanent feature of ongoing process operations. Documentation is updated and **training** is performed as needed to ensure that the **change** is fully integrated into daily operations.

The PDCA cycle is sometimes called the *Shewhart cycle* and the *Deming cycle*—Walter **Shewhart** developed the concept and described it in his book *Statistical Methods from the Viewpoint of Quality Control* (Washington, D.C.: The Graduate School, Department of Agriculture, 1939), and W. Edwards **Deming** popularized the concept in Japan.

planned grouping   This term refers to those methods associated with improving the sensitivity of **experimental designs** through the use of specially designed experimental patterns. Examples include block designs, matched pair designs, and repeated measures designs.

planning, extrapolation   See **extrapolation planning**.

planning phase (phase II)   This is the second phase of a TQM implementation program. (See the Introduction of this publication for an overview of all five phases.) This phase consists of these basic steps:

1. *Securing of commitment.* Secure commitment of the estimated resources required in order to validate the commitment level of the company to these changes and lay the foundation for real progress.

2. *Establishing the TQM implementation organization and infrastructure.*
   A. A business lead team is established and a **facilitator** is assigned to lead regular meetings. The lead team's role is to lead the **policy deployment** activities throughout the organization. This involves constructing a workable plan and committing adequate resources over a sufficient period of time to see the company through the implementation process. The lead team is comprised of senior-level executives from the entire organization, including repre-

sentatives of organized labor when they are a part of the operation. They should provide a sense of legitimacy, importance, and structure to the TQM program.

B. A steering committee that represents a cross-section of the company's employee base is established. The role of committee members is to facilitate the implementation of TQM throughout the organization. They do this by providing both horizontal linkage between improvement **teams** and senior management, and horizontal linkage (in a process form) between functional organizations. The steering committee identifies those improvement projects that are likely to have the greatest impact on the organization and the greatest likelihood of success. Committee members then charter the process improvement teams to perform these improvements, providing guidance, resources, and technical assistance as required. They set specific targets and metrics for improvement as each team is chartered and monitor progress toward those targets, taking **corrective action** as needed. They also provide regular, comprehensive status on overall improvement progress to the business lead team. (See **chartering a team**.)

C. Process improvement teams (PITs) are established, chartered, and guided by the steering committee, as described in the previous text. They are comprised of process experts from each of the functional areas involved in the process that is targeted for improvement. Teams may also include **suppliers** and **customers**. PITs are temporary in nature and disband when projects are complete.

3. *Strategic planning and **policy deployment**.*
    A. **Mission statements** are reviewed when they exist and adjusted as required to reflect the importance of meeting **customer needs** and utilizing TQM principles in that pursuit.
    B. A **vision** of the future state of the business is generated—a vision that is compelling and desirable to all company **stakeholders**.
    C. Company **goals** and **objectives** are defined or modified to reflect the mission and vision statement(s) generated in

the previous steps. The goals and objectives should provide specific targets for improvement initiatives and tactical planning and should incorporate the anticipated impact on the bottom line (return on investment). No fewer than three and no more than seven goals and objectives should be stated to retain adequate focus through the course of the initial round of TQM implementation. The output of this process should be the backbone of the company's operating or **business plan**.

4. *Development of the implementation plan.* Planning should then be done to determine which specific processes will need to be improved to attain the specific goals and objectives defined previously. Planning will identify timing and steps involved in the deployment of process improvement teams, and high-level monitoring and reporting milestones. Planning should also include a cursory cost/benefit analysis and an estimation of required resources for the completion of each major improvement initiative.

5. *Awareness training.*
   A. The impacts of a total quality philosophy are discussed and described in detail, based on information from case studies of similar implementations and popular TQM press. The costs as well as the potential benefits are outlined so that expectations and anticipated commitments are understood as clearly as possible.
   B. Principles and practices of TQM are then described, usually by an outside consultant who has led other organizations through the process. A basic understanding of the TQM tools and techniques and their applications is realized in this step, so that management understands the terminology and process elements that will become a regular part of the **company's culture**.
   C. The importance and role of the customer are reviewed and explored in some detail, focusing on the (internal and external) customer as the definer of *quality,* and as an integral part of the improvement process.
   D. Commitment and **ownership** are established by involving all of the participants of both the business lead team and the steering committee in the development and implementation planning activities. Specific improvement tar-

gets and time frames are tied directly to the reward structure of these employees, and they are required to state their commitment or withdraw from the process. See also **reward and recognition system**.

plateau distribution   A **distribution** of values measured and plotted in chart form, which looks like a hill with a flat top and no really discernible peak. This form of distribution typically has slight tails on each end of the distribution and is most often the result of multiple **bell-shaped distributions** with centers roughly evenly distributed throughout the range shown on the chart. See Figure 37. See also **kurtosis**.

platykurtic   See **kurtosis**.

PLC   See **programmable logic controller.**

point-of-use inspection   **Inspection** performed by the user (downstream internal customer) at the point where the part is used (typically where the part is installed in the next assembly) in a manufacturing operation.

Poisson distribution   A probability **distribution** for discrete random variables that can take integer (whole) values (**ordinal data**). See Figure 38. It takes the form

$$P^{(X)} = \frac{\lambda^x}{x!} e^{-\lambda}$$

poka-yoke   A Japanese term that refers to **foolproofing** a design such that all ambiguity is removed and it becomes virtually impossible to

Figure 37. **Plateau distribution.**

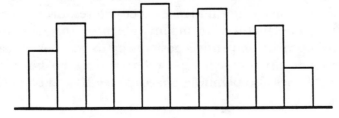

Figure 38. **Poisson distribution for average = 1, 5, 10, 20.**

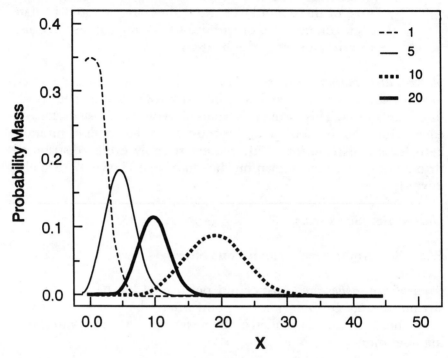

set up a machine or produce a part or an assembly incorrectly. This is often accomplished through designing the components of the tools and the assemblies so they will fit together only in the proper orientation and sequence.

policy   A statement of principle that exists to direct a specific course of action by the employees of a company.

policy deployment   One of three integrated **quality** management subsystems supporting **total quality management (TQM)**. It is an integrated strategic planning process in which a company develops and deploys three to five major initiatives, focusing resources on a critical few (usually one to three) companywide breakthrough areas required to improve competitive position or to counter threats in a social/economic environment. Also referred to as **hoshin planning**. See Figure 39. See also **planning phase (phase II)** and **breakthrough improvements**.

Figure 39. The fundamental elements of policy deployment.

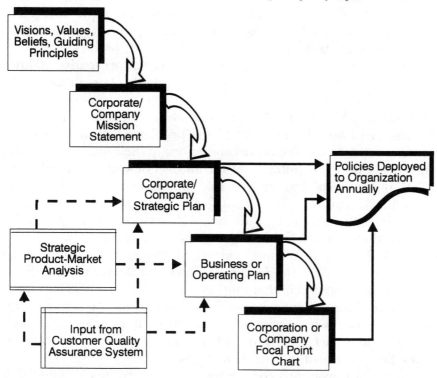

population A collection of all identifiable observations in accordance with a set of rules or **boundaries**. Also called a *target population* or *universe,* the term *population* refers to the aggregate of all observations of interest to the researcher. In this case, the term *of interest* refers to the total set of observations to which the researcher wishes to generalize the results of the research study. See also **research population**.

PPM See **parts per million**.

precision The relative degree of agreement among repeated and reproduced individual measurements or test results for one or more measurement processes or systems. The components of variation for precision are associated with **repeatability** and **reproducibility**. The degree of precision in a measurement process is generally designated as the standard deviation of measurement error, or σ_E. See also **accuracy**.

predictive maintenance   Within a TQM environment, the use of an array of statistical models and methods intended to signal **corrective action** to a **process** before associated critical product variables can move out of **control**. In a more limited context, predictive maintenance is also used to describe the performance of **preventive maintenance** in a predictive, rather than reactive, mode of operation.

preparation phase (phase I)   The period when executives examine the nature of their businesses and the problems that must be overcome in order to become more competitive in their markets. (See the Introduction of this publication for an overview of all five phases.) TQM is one such strategy that may be applied across industries. Nonetheless, executive-level management must consider the range of possible strategies in light of their business environment and decide for themselves whether TQM is the approach that they should embrace. Management must understand the magnitude of **change** (not merely physical and **process** changes, but the far more difficult cultural changes as well) that must occur in a successful TQM implementation. This self-examination is best done with the help of a top consulting **team** who is trusted by executive management and has a demonstrated track record with a broad range of improvement strategies. See also **consultant's role in TQM**.

It is not uncommon for the top management team to establish or reestablish its **vision** and **mission statements** for the company during this phase. At the very least, they should be carefully reviewed as management tries to determine the future goals of the company and why they have been selected.

Finally, the culmination of the preparation phase should be commitment to an approach, and if management decides to proceed with TQM, the next four phases of implementation should be undertaken. Management must understand, however, that commitment to TQM means that the entire philosophy and culture of the company will necessarily change. (See **company culture**.) The company must orient itself toward process-based management, process **control**, and continuous process improvement with one overriding **objective**: satisfaction of **customer needs**, and eventually, satisfying those needs even before the customer clearly understands what they are! The **leadership** of TQM implementation cannot be delegated. TQM implementation must be led by top management in a lead-by-example manner.

prevention   Avoidance of nonconformances in products and services; not allowing an error or **defect** to occur. It takes many forms depending on the application involved, but all of its forms involve reducing **variability**. See also **detection vs. prevention, prevention costs, nonconformity**, and **conformance**.

prevention costs   Those costs incurred because of action taken to prevent errors or **defects**, lowering or eliminating the other two categories of the **cost of quality**: **appraisal costs** and **failure** costs. Prevention costs include education and **training** costs, **design review** costs, and process **control**-related costs. See also **education and training (for total quality)**.

preventive maintenance   All actions performed in an attempt to retain an item in its specified condition by providing systematic **inspection, detection**, and **prevention** of developing **failures**. See also **detection vs. prevention**.

price (as relates to cost)   See **cost-price model**.

prioritizing improvements   It is common during the **planning phase** of a TQM implementation to identify several potential improvement projects to be undertaken, all of which offer some benefit to the company. Prioritizing these opportunities correctly involves mapping each potential improvement to the associated critical business performance metrics, as defined with the identification of critical **business processes**. A matrix may be constructed, listing opportunities along the Y axis, and critical business performance metrics along the X axis. Then each opportunity may be rated by the business lead team as having a high, medium, or low impact on each metric. A further refinement that adds value to this analysis is rating each business metric in terms of its relative importance. In this manner, a medium impact improvement on a metric with a value of "10" would be undertaken before an opportunity that was determined to have a high impact on a metric that is only valued at "2," assuming that higher numbers rank more highly in terms of their importance. In this manner, the cumulative positive effect of each opportunity may readily be compared to all other opportunities, and priorities should become clear. See also **comparative and relative importance**.

Prize, Deming   See **Deming Prize**.

problem-solving strategy (PSS)   Working toward a solution to a problem. While there are several problem-solving approaches in use by TQM practitioners, a good example is the technique employed by Florida Power & Light when seeking the **Deming Prize**. This approach follows the steps of the **PDCA** process:

Plan

1. *Reasons for improvement*. Adopt team mission that defines the improvement theme (general problem). Document importance and why problem should be worked on. Schedule problem-solving activities.
2. *Current situation*. Understand the nature of the problem. Select appropriate components of the theme (subproblem) for improvement. Set an improvement target.
3. *Analysis*. Identify and verify the **root causes** of the problem or undesired state.

Do

4. *Countermeasures*. Select and implement countermeasures that will counteract the root causes of the problem.

Check

5. *Results*. Check the effectiveness of the countermeasures. Determine if problem correction or desired change has been achieved. If not, return to step 3.

Act

6. *Standardization*. Prevent the problem from recurring. Standardize and achieve **control** to maintain the gains. (See also **standardization** and **standard operating procedure**.)
7. *Future plans*. Plan what to do about any remaining problems and evaluate the team's effectiveness.

process   Any repetitive series of events. Generally, the use of the term *process* (versus *activity* or *operation*) implies that the events are operating in a state of statistical control and are therefore affected by only **common causes** of variation, rendering the output of the events stable and predictable. See also **control (statistical)**.

process, business   See **business processes**.

process, support   See **support processes.**

process capability   The degree to which the **process** (output) meets (will meet) **specifications** or requirements on an ongoing basis. Capability refers to the future performance of the process, not to its past or present performance, although past or current data are used in making the assessment of capability. The prediction of future performance requires stability and predictability in the process output. Therefore, *actual* or *true* capability cannot be assessed until the process has been documented to be in a state of **control**. If the process is not in a state of control, any calculation of capability must be called *potential* capability, and in most cases should not be calculated at all. See also **in-control process** and **out-of-control process.**

Proper calculations of capability consider both process **variability** (spread) and process **central tendency** (center). In many cases, variability and closeness to a proper target, as opposed to being centered between the specifications, must be considered. It is for these reasons that there are at least three commonly used indices of capability: C_p, C_{pk}, and C_{pm}. Since the C_p index accounts only for variability (and not centrality or location), one or both of the other indices are used along with C_p.

C_p is an index that is the ratio of the spread across the specification (total **tolerance** or **upper specification limit** minus the **lower specification limit**) to the spread across the process distribution (the center 99.73% of the process **distribution**, also called the **natural tolerance**). For a **normal distribution**, the spread across the middle 99.73% is represented as **six sigma** or 6σ (which can be estimated from **control charts** by R-bar/d_2 or S-bar/c_4). This value can also be obtained by subtracting the lower natural process limit (LNPL) from the upper natural process limit (UNPL). For the nonnormal case, the spread across the middle 99.73% of the process distribution is obtained by distributional fitting methods. In either case the following holds for C_p:

$$C_p = \frac{(USL - LSL)}{(UNPL - LNPL)}$$

and for normal distributions, the simplification for C_p is:

$$C_p = \frac{(USL - LSL)}{6\sigma}$$

C_p can take on values from 0 to $+\infty$.

The C_{pk} index considers not only process variability, but also the degree of centering. C_{pk} can be understood as decreasing the value of C_p as a function of the degree to which the process average deviates from the center of the specification limits. Indeed, an initial formula for C_{pk} was:

$$C_{pk} = C_p (1 - k) \text{ where } k = \frac{|\mu - spec\ midpoint|}{\left(\dfrac{USL - LSL}{2}\right)}$$

Another more popular and easy-to-follow calculation for C_{pk} involves the use of **z-scores** calculated for the specification limit values relative to the process distribution. A z-score is calculated for the USL called Z_U and for the LSL called Z_L. The absolute values of these two z-scores are taken and the smaller of the two is used in calculating C_{pk} as follows:

$$C_{pk} = \frac{\min[|Z_u|'|Z_l|]}{3}$$

And an alternative formula for C_{pk} is:

$$C_{pk} = \frac{(\mu - Nearest\ Specification\ Limit)}{3\sigma}$$

The above calculations for C_{pk} are predicated upon the condition of normality in the process distribution. If this is not the case, the above values will be incorrect and one should use an alternative such as the equivalent C_{pk}.

The equivalent C_{pk} index (called $C_{pk}{}^E$) can be obtained if one is able to estimate the percent of observations expected to be **out of specification** for the particular nonnormal process distribution. In that case, the largest proportion (percent) out of specification is determined, that proportion is taken to the unit normal table, and an estimated z-score is retrieved and treated as an estimate of the minimum z in the following formula:

$$C_{pk}^E = \frac{\hat{Z}\text{min}}{3}$$

The value of C_{pk} (and C_{pk}^E) relative to C_p is given in the following expression: $0 \leq C_{pk} \leq C_p$. Some practitioners use a negative C_{pk} value when the process average is outside of the specification limits, but in actuality C_{pk} is undefined in such a case.

C_{pm} is an index of capability that takes into consideration both process variability and deviation of the process average from the target (or nominal) value. Therefore, it is an index that reveals total variability or deviation from the target or nominal. When the target is centered between the specification limits, C_{pm} gives information about all of the process data relative to the target and in that sense is more informative than C_{pk}, although C_{pk} is usually calculated.

C_{pm} is computed as follows:

$$C_{pm} = \frac{C_p}{\sqrt{1 + \frac{(\mu - N_o)^2}{\sigma^2}}} = \frac{(USL - LSL)}{6\sqrt{\sigma^2 + (\mu - N_o)^2}}$$

where N_o is the nominal or target value.

The value of C_{pm} relative to C_p is $0 \leq C_{pm} \leq C_p$. It should be noted that C_{pm} is almost always less than C_{pk}, but there are cases when C_{pm} could be greater than C_{pk}.

The capability ratio (CR) is the spread across the process distribution divided by the spread across the specification and is the reciprocal of the C_p index.

process capability index   A calculated value that provides an indication of the degree to which the **process** output is expected to meet **specification**. Most index values are defined in such a way that a marginally capable process has an index of 1.0 and increasing index values indicate increased capability as with C_p, C_{pk}, C_{pm}, P_{pk}, and P_{pm}, etc. (An index of less than 1.0 means that the process is not capable.)

However, the capability ratio (CR) indicates increased capability with values smaller than 1.0. See also **process capability**.

process change   See **change**.

process characteristics   See **critical process characteristics**.

process/equipment reliability   A look at the probability that equipment or a process will function as intended. Manufacturing systems and mechanical equipment are subject to **failures** that may be classified into three basic groups:

1. *Infant mortality*. Usually associated with new or renewed equipment, the result of improperly installed equipment, or extremely low-life components due to manufacturing variations.
2. *Random*. Unreliable design, insufficient redundancy, unexpected and unpredictable occurrences, or product misuse.
3. *Wearout*. Predictable and limited to age or cycle.

See also **reliability** and **reliability modeling**.

process improvement team (PIT)   See **planning phase (phase II)**.

process-oriented flow   An approach to the layout of the workplace that organizes the work in a way that reflects the **processes** that the work goes through. Similar to the *focus factory* approach, the principle of process-oriented flow is based on generic routings for entire families of parts. This approach is in sharp contrast to the **functional layout**, which is more traditional, especially in manufacturing companies. Traditional functional approaches group similar equipment in the same geographic areas of the workplace, which requires the work to be moved repeatedly over long distances in order to perform the operations required for transformation. The process-oriented approach locates all of the equipment and tools required through the production routing in close physical proximity, regardless of equipment type. This allows for minimal throughput times and **work-in-process** inventory. See also **just-in-time manufacturing** and **parts flow**.

process-oriented plant layout   See **process-oriented flow**.

process planning, automated   See **automated process planning**.

process value analysis (PVA)   A phase in the implementation of **activity-based costing** in which a **process** is studied and analyzed to determine the level of value added. This would likely involve:

- Observing a process and recording a listing of each process step.
- Identifying the resources required to complete each step (e.g., time, manpower, and floor space).
- Assessing each step to determine which steps add value to the product or service rendered.
- Assessing what level of value added is for the process as a whole.

process variables   The various conditions and settings at the operation that influence product **quality**. Process variables may include:

time	temperature	machine speed
pressure	clearances	tooling dimensions
tension	flow settings	tooling surface conditions
recipes/formulas	dwell times	ramp times
roller positions	tooling heights	vacuum pressures

See also **critical process characteristics** and **quality tables**.

procurement costs   See **total cost concept in purchasing**.

procurement technology, advanced   See **advanced procurement technology**.

product characteristics   The various conditions and measurements of the product that describe the **quality** of the product. Product characteristics include such elements as:

size	weight	color
strength	hardness	print-to-cut

surface condition	**defect** level	register
resistivity	turn on voltage	moisture of product

See also **critical product characteristics** and **quality tables**.

product market analysis   See **strategic product market analysis**.

production validation   A series of tests and appraisals performed to assure that initial production parts will meet the design intent. Typically, production validation includes the following elements:

1. Ensure that all requirements are included in engineering specifications.
2. Conduct functional tests and durability tests.
3. Complete all requirements before initial shipment.
4. Include all **sample sizes** and acceptance criteria.
5. Obtain concurrence from manufacturing and **quality control** through feasibility reviews.
6. Rerun the first five steps when processes or designs change.

profit, short-term   A metric that has motivated management to operate under a short time horizon when it comes to profit planning. Many CEOs and CFOs believe that capital investment diminishes the price of company stock, is too costly, and leads to unfavorable depreciation requirements. These executives think that capital investment is detrimental to their own careers and should be minimized. The result of this approach is undercapitalized companies with large cash reserves in paper investment vehicles and deliberate, forced obsolescence of the business. This is particularly true in manufacturing companies.

TQM is at odds with this philosophy, not because TQM advocates large capital investments (it usually does not), but because the heart of TQM is a long-range view that **quality** will bring about growth through **continuous improvement**. That improvement often causes the need for capital investment in an incremental manner. Furthermore, more significant expenditures are sometimes made together with just-in-time implementations, moving equipment, and reconfiguring factory floor operations. This conflict between short-term profitability and long-term growth and sustainability is a long-standing problem and is only exacerbated when senior-level managers do not recognize the long-range nature of a commitment to TQM.

profound knowledge, a system of A phrase coined by Dr. W. Edwards **Deming** to describe the underlying foundation from which the **14 points** follow as application and to provide a working theory in order to understand and optimize organizations. This system is made up of four component parts, each related to the others: appreciation for a system, knowledge about variation, theory of knowledge, and psychology.

program evaluation and review technique (PERT) A project management tool that produces a **flow chart** depicting the sequences and interdependencies of critical activities in the project. The output chart from this process enables users to quickly identify the critical path (the longest sequential string) of activities through the project, keeping attention focused on the most important progressive steps. (See **critical path method**.) The PERT process includes the following steps:

1. *Identify all of the significant activities in the project.* Then establish milestones that represent their completion.
2. *Identify the sequence in which these activities must be performed.* This is usually accomplished most easily by working backward, identifying interdependencies and completion times for each step. For example, before the last step is performed (usually packaging or shipping), determine what other steps must be completed. Before these steps are performed, see what other steps must be completed, and so on.
3. *Develop the flow chart.* The activity completion milestones are each represented by numbered or labeled "bubbles," with connecting lines representing the dependencies between the activities. Each line should be identified with a number that represents the time to do this work, or the entire diagram may be plotted on a time-based scale, with the weeks called out along the bottom of the chart.
4. *Count the number of weeks in each "string" of interdependent activities.* (Actually the time increment is irrelevant. It could be minutes, weeks, months, or years.) This way the critical path may be identified for the attention of the project managers.

5. *Maintain the chart*. Since the actual work time required always varies from estimated times, the actual critical path will shift back and forth between lengthening and shortening strings of activity.

programmable logic controller (PLC)   A computer used to control process **variability** through machine adjustment based on preloaded computer instructions. PLCs are usually RISC (reduced instruction set computing) based and are applied to machines performing repetitive work in industrial environments.

project plan development   The most important step in the **planning phase (phase II)** of a TQM implementation. The project plan must be comprehensive, realistic, and reflective of the **goals** and **objectives** of the company as it focuses on satisfying **customer needs**. The development of project plans will flow from **policy deployment** when deploying the **strategic plan** of the company.

PSS   See **problem-solving strategy**.

pull signals   Devices used to signal the prior operators that they are authorized to produce another unit. Pull signals may be as sophisticated as electronic messages on a computer screen or as simple as an empty spot in the previous operation's outgoing area.

pull system   A way of managing shop floor (or even office-level) activity that minimizes **work-in-process** and dramatically improves throughput time by eliminating interoperation queues. A pull system requires two things: a **pull signal** and a fixed upper volume limit. A fixed upper volume limit means that operators must stop producing parts whenever they have not received their (pull signal) authorization to produce more. If only two pull signal devices are provided between operations, then a maximum of two parts will exist in flow between those operations at any given point in time. Pull signals are sometimes called **kanbans**. See also **push systems**.

push systems   The antithesis of the **pull system**. Push systems allow production to continue based on a predetermined schedule. Push systems launch orders into the production system on a scheduled interval and assume that they will come out the end of the **process** at the end of the designated throughput times. Even the best closed-loop push systems are much less responsive to in-process variation, and therefore much less effective for controlling production and **work-in-process** than pull systems.

Q

QA See **quality assurance**.

QFD See **quality function deployment**.

QIS See **quality improvement strategy**.

quality The never-ending reduction of variation around a customer-defined target in the absence of **defects**. **Customers** most often define quality in terms of the product or service's attributes that are most important to them. The most readily perceivable evidence of quality is the satisfaction of customer requirements the first time and every time the product or service is used. See also **big Q, little q**.

quality, average outgoing See **average outgoing quality**.

quality, conformance See **conformance quality**.

quality, definitions of The ways **quality** is defined. **Juran** defines quality as **fitness for use** and **Deming** defines it as follows: "Improvement of the **process**, which increases uniformity of output of product, reduces rework and mistakes, reduces **waste** of manpower, machine-time, and materials, and thus increases output with less effort." The most important thing to remember about definitions of quality is that they are only relevant to the extent that they provide **value** to the **customer**, as perceived by the customer.

quality, design See **design quality**.

quality (as related to cost and schedule) See **cost/schedule/quality relationship**.

quality assurance (QA) All activities essential to ensuring that a product or service will meet the needs of an internal or external customer. See **customer, external**, **customer, internal**, and **customer needs**.

quality assurance, customer See **customer quality assurance**.

quality assurance, total See **total quality assurance**.

quality assurance organization, functions of The functions of the quality assurance organization shift dramatically with the implementation of TQM. There are several categories of these **changes**, including:

1. *Quality's target.* Where the QA organization's target shifts from **conformance** to requirements to minimal variation from **target values**.
2. *Quality planning.* Where the function of QA shifts from defining the minimum requirements for product and **process** measurements to **quality function deployment**.
3. *Defining acceptability.* Where the shift is away from defining what is acceptable and toward **continuous improvement**.
4. *Cost reduction.* Where emphasis shifts away from reducing **failure** costs toward reducing overall process variation in order to drive down total costs of nonquality.
5. *Inspection.* Where the emphasis shifts away from inspection by the QA organization toward operator-based process **control** with occasional QA **audits**.
6. *Responsibility.* Where the responsibility for quality shifts away from QA and toward every individual for the quality of his or her own work.

quality characteristic See **satisfier**.

quality circles Groups of people who meet regularly (sometimes with their supervisors) to identify and solve **quality**-related problems within their **processes**. Quality circles reached their peak in terms of quantity in the 1980s. More recently, these efforts have shifted into other mediums such as process improvement **teams** and **natural work groups**. The primary activities performed by the **quality circle** include detailed process definition (including identification of the internal and external **customers**), elimination of non-value-added activity in the processes, and establishment of performance baselines and targets. Quality circles typically are composed of three to nine employees who work in the same geographic area, most often operating equipment within a defined sequential process.

quality control   The operational methods and activities used to fulfill **quality** requirements, usually through and including the evaluation of data. Quality control, in the "old school," was the name given to the department responsible for product **inspection.** See also **statistical quality control**.

quality control circles   See **quality circles**.

quality dissatisfiers/deficiencies   See **dissatisfier**.

quality function deployment (QFD)   A method used to translate **customer** needs into appropriate technical requirements for every stage of product development—from the concept stage through distribution. The QFD process begins with a step often called "listening to the voice of the customer." The American Supplier Institute has defined QFD as "a system for translating consumer requirements into appropriate company requirements at each stage from research and product development to engineering and manufacturing to marketing/sales and **distribution**.

QFD uses a table called the **house of quality**, which has several "rooms" defining the relationships between design requirements and **customer** requirements (the "what" room); the relationship between what the company does and its satisfaction of design requirements (the "how" room); objective **target values** (the "how much" room); and both engineering and customer competitive assessments.

QFD is usually implemented in four phases:

1. *Product planning*. Design requirements are matched to **customer needs**, allowing the critical design requirements to be identified.
2. *Part deployment*. Part **characteristics** are matched to critical design requirements identified in step 1, allowing the critical part characteristics to be identified.
3. *Process planning*. Process operations are matched to critical part characteristics, allowing key process operations to be identified.
4. *Production planning*. Key production operations are matched against production requirements to identify the operations that

must be brought into tight process **control** in order to result in **customer satisfaction**.

See also **quality tables**.

quality improvement strategy (QIS)   A disciplined plan for the application of statistical tools for bringing a critical product **characteristic** into a state of **control**, capability, and/or acceptability.

quality level, acceptable   See **acceptable quality level**.

quality loss function   A parabolic approximation of the monetary cost and quality loss that results when a quality **characteristic (satisfier)** does not meet its **target value**. The cost of this deviation increases quadratically as the quality characteristic moves farther away from its target. The quality loss function was first introduced in this form by Genichi **Taguchi**, and the formula used to compute it varies depending on the type of quality characteristic being observed. See **Taguchi loss function**.

quality management, absolutes of   See **absolutes of quality management**.

quality management systems   Systems composed of effective, comprehensive plans; strong TQM **leadership** at every level of the organization that has "bought in" to TQM as a way of life; discrete metrics that accurately reflect **process** health and provide the basis for **continuous improvement**; and active continuous improvement toward **customer satisfaction**. See also **planning phase (phase II)** and **implementation phase (phase IV)**.

quality management values   Among the values most successful TQM organizations hold are:

1. Open, honest **communication** with employees, **customers**, and **suppliers**
2. Absolute faith in the concept that **customer satisfaction** equates to **quality**, and that quality equates to success
3. Measurable, discrete performance **goals** at every level, **benchmarked** against the best in that business

4. Realism, and the recognition that TQM is a lifetime commitment, not a quick-fix plan for improving short-term profitability

See also **organizational values**.

quality planning, advanced   See **advanced quality planning**.

quick-change devices   Devices used in manufacturing setup reduction activities to eliminate the adjustments required during setup changeovers. Among the devices most commonly used on manufacturing equipment are quick-change couplings, clamps, locator pins, and fixed-position stops for dies and fixtures.

R

R chart   Range chart. A common type of **control chart** used with continuous (or variables) data to evaluate the **stability** of the range (R) of **subgroup** samples with subgroup size less than 8. The results may also be used to estimate the overall process variance. The R chart should be accompanied by an $\bar{X}$ chart or an $\tilde{X}$ (median) chart to show central **tendency**.

R_M chart   Moving range chart. A **control chart** that usually accompanies an **X chart** and reflects variation in the process by plotting the range between each value and the previous value.

RAB   See **Registrar Accreditation Board**.

radar chart   See **spider chart**.

random sampling   The selection of size **n** units from a **population** where each **sample** has an equal chance of being selected.

randomization   The process of assigning experimental units to treatment conditions, or the order of testing, in a purely chance manner. Typically, randomization is associated with three **experimental design** functions:

1. **Random sampling** or selection
2. Random assignment
3. Randomization of order

R&R studies   See **gauge repeatability and reproducibility (studies)**.

range chart   See **R chart**.

ratio data   An interval data scale, structured such that the ratio between any two measures results in a meaningful metric. See also **continuous data** and **variables data**.

reaction plan   Accompanied by an associated **control chart**, a plan that details what the empowered process owner is to do, check, and act upon should the monitored process go "out of control." Specific reactions corresponding to the nature of the out-of-control conditions, which may appear, should be identified in the reaction plan whenever possible. See also **out-of-control process**.

recovery   Good output from the operation divided by the total output from the operation. Also known as *yield*.

red bead experiment   An experiment developed by Dr. W. Edwards **Deming** to demonstrate that managers should not rank employees based on previous performance because observed performance differences may well be attributed to the system, not the employees. In this experiment, 4000 beads (20% red, 80% white) are placed in a jar and stirred, and then six people each select a **sample** of 50 beads. Each person's goal is to produce white beads, because the **customer** will reject red beads. When everyone has a sample, the red beads are counted. The limits of the variation between the six individuals that can be attributed to the system are calculated and each will likely fall within these calculated limits. The calculations illustrate that there is no real evidence that one person will be a better performer than another in the future, so it would be a **waste** of management's time to try to determine why, for example, Susan produced eight red beads and Bob produced twelve. Instead, the red bead experiment demonstrates that management should work to improve the system, allowing everyone to improve performance.

Registrar Accreditation Board (RAB)   A private, nonprofit organization that ensures the competence of **quality** systems registrars. Their method involves providing accreditation to international standards for the registrars.

registration, ISO 9000   The presence of a supplier in the registration listing of an accredited registrar, following the conferring of "registered" status by that registrar. See also **ISO 9000** and **certification, ISO 9000**.

registration, (ISO) registrar The presence of a registrar in the listing of accredited registrars maintained by the **Registrar Accreditation Board**.

relationship diagram A chart developed to assist in the **problem-solving** process and one of the **seven basic tools of quality**. The diagram depicts the relationships between naturally grouped sets of problems and ideas. In using a relationship diagram, the process improvement **team**:

1. Writes each problem (or symptom) in a circle.
2. Draws arrows between the circles showing the influence of one idea on the others (Solid line arrows mean strong influence and are counted as a value of "1." Dotted lines represent weak influence, and are represented by values of ".5").
3. Ranks the circles by the cumulative influence value emanating from each circle, and the circles with the highest value are targeted first for resolution.

See also **affinity diagram**.

reliability The probability that a system, production center, machine, or component will perform its intended function (in a stated condition or environment) for a predetermined period of time without **failure**. Reliability of a system is indicated by R_s. See also **process/equipment reliability**.

reliability, information Information reliability has a direct impact on the **customer's** perception of the **quality** of the product when it misleads customers as to the use of the product, the maintenance of the product, the specifications of the product, or other factors that may become **dissatisfiers**. See also **expectations, customer**.

reliability, tooling See **tooling reliability**.

reliability modeling Application of different mathematical models to identify the probability of **failure** in a system. **Reliability** may be thought of as a "bathtub curve," when it is viewed as a function of time, spread over the life cycle of the system. See Figure 40. During the *startup* phase of any system, the failure rate is high, and comes down a steep curve until it flattens out sharply during the mature *useful life* portion of the system's life cycle, then accelerates steeply

Figure 40. **Reliability bathtub curve.**

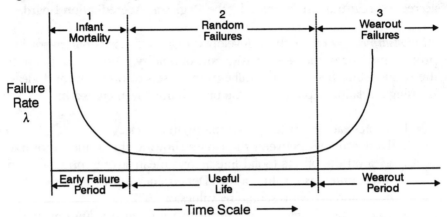

again in the later *wearout* period at the end of the system's life cycle. Since the middle period or useful life period is much longer than either of the other two periods, the graphing of this failure probability curve produces the "bathtub" look, and hence the name. At these different stages, and depending on the nature and quantity of the equipment involved in the process, different mathematical models may be utilized to determine the reliability level of the system. The exponential model, the reliability series, the reliability of parallel systems series, and the k-out-of-n system are among the reliability models employed. See also **process/equipment reliability**.

reliability prediction   Quantitative assessments of **reliability**. These predictions are used by engineers to assess the reliability of systems and subsystems, facilitate trade-offs between reliability and other factors, and forecast system and subsystem performance over time. In the case of existing systems, the reliability of the system may be assessed by establishing a base **failure** rate, breaking this failure rate down into manageable elements, and adjusting the elements to reflect changes. In the case of completely new designs, the approach used will require a combination of some of the following elements:

1. **Failure modes and effects analysis**
2. Comparison of new design components with similar components and failure modes of existing designs
3. Laboratory testing
4. Subcomponent testing

repeatability   The ability of a measurement process to show close agreement among a number of consecutive measurements of the same unit being measured under the same operating conditions. The **variability** of measurement within a single measurement system.

replication   The acquisition of two or more observations under a set of identical experimental conditions, or the collection of multiple observations under a set of identical experimental conditions, or the collection of multiple observations at each of the treatment conditions tested. The primary purpose of replication is to provide quantifiable and accurate measurement of the **precision** of the design, where precision relates to the concept of experimental error.

reproducibility   The ability of a measurement process to show close agreement among repeated measurements of the same unit being measured by multiple measurement processes or systems contributing to a single process stream. The **variability** of **measurement error** between measurement systems.

requirements planning   See **distribution requirements planning**.

research population   That portion of the **population** or universe available for **sampling**.

resistance, planning for   Identifying anticipated areas of resistance to TQM implementation and broad-brush planning for dealing with that resistance. This planning should occur in the first two phases of the TQM implementation. Specific planning should also be done in the third and fourth phases, as process improvement **teams** are chartered and deployed. (See **chartering a team**.) Resistance to **change** is often the single most commonly cited reason for the **failure** of TQM programs, after lack of top management support. Resistance to change may be most effectively mitigated in the following ways:

1. Proactive management that communicates honestly and openly about the changes in expectations and the importance of those changes. See also **communication**.
2. Changes in measurements, particularly performance measurements, in a way that supports the new ways of doing business.

3. Movement from vertical organization to horizontal, process-based organization. This will more effectively communicate that the process, and **control** of **variability** in the process, are now of paramount importance to management.
4. **Empowerment** and involvement of employees at every level of the organization in the development and deployment of change. See also **employee involvement**.

resolution   The smallest increment or unit of measure available from a measurement process.

resource infrastructure   The network of people and systems from which resources are drawn for process improvement efforts. These resources include people, equipment, materials, facilities, dollars, time, and information.

resource matrix   A matrix that compares available resources (typically in man-hours) to the time required to perform functional responsibilities, achieve strategic objectives (focal point items), and maintain critical tactical items.

response variable   See **dependent variable**.

reward and recognition system   A component of **employee involvement**. Employee ideas and efforts (e.g., **problem-solving, quality** improvement) should be recognized, regardless of their outcome. This recognition may consist of:

1. A personal visit by management to the employee's work area to congratulate him or her and express sincere appreciation
2. Selection for presentation at a quarterly **quality** review session
3. Posting the employee's name on the company bulletin board in the implementation area, so that others can express their appreciation for the employee's efforts
4. Monetary awards, trips, and so forth, for the suggestions that generate the best improvement results, or that enhance employee safety

risk   The probability of making an error while testing a **hypothesis**. See also **Type I error** and **Type II error**.

risk sharing An approach to new product development that involves suppliers' assuming some part of the risk in the new product development and launch by investing in their own start-up costs in return for some end-product profits. See also **strategic alliances**.

risks of TQM The risks involved with implementing TQM in any business. Among the most frequently experienced risks are:

1. The drag on resources required to implement such a comprehensive program while still running the day-to-day business.
2. The long time horizon for return on investment. (See **profits, short-term**.)
3. The fear of **change**, resulting in some near-term upheaval, dissension, and disruption. (See **planning for resistance**.)
4. Disintegration occurring between **processes** as only a few are improved at a time.

Recognizing and anticipating these factors will go a long way toward enabling management to effectively reduce the risks associated with these factors.

robustness Aspects or **characteristics** of a product or **process** that remain relatively stable (exhibit minimum variation levels), even though factors that influence operations or usage, such as environment and wear, are constantly changing. See also **stability**.

root cause The most fundamental reasons (causes) that requirements are not met. Identifying root causes often requires "peeling back" the reasons first expressed when looking at the ultimate symptom of a problem. For example, poor paint finish may be caused by problems with paint adherence. Problems with paint adherence may be caused by hydraulic fluid leaks. Hydraulic fluid leaks may be caused by loose connections. Loose connections in hydraulic lines may be caused by poor tightening methods or tools.

run An out-of-control condition identified on a **control chart** as eight or more consecutive points on one side of the center line (i.e., at least eight consecutive points above or eight consecutive points below the center line). A run indicates that a **special cause** of variation is present that has caused a shift in the process average. See also **out-of-control process**.

run chart   A graph depicting consecutive measures plotted around the center line.

S

s-chart A **standard deviation** chart. A type of **control chart** involving the **subgroup standard deviation**, s, which is used to evaluate the **stability** of the **variability** within the **process**. Usually accompanies an **X-bar chart** and is used when the subgroup is greater than or equal to 8.

sample A portion or subset of a **population** or to take a sample.

sample size The number of experimental units, objects, or subjects in a **sample** or **subgroup.**

sampling, random See **random sampling.**

sampling error The expected and quantifiable discrepancy between a statistic and its associated **parameter** due to the **sample size** and the **variability** of the **population** from which the **sample** was drawn. Also sometimes called *chance*.

SAPPHO Project A study conducted by the University of Sussex in Brighton, Great Britain, which paired successful innovators with unsuccessful innovators who were seeking similar **innovations**. The study showed that the most significant difference between success levels of the innovations developed was the level of attention paid to identifying and understanding **customer needs**. SAPPHO is an acronym for Scientific Activity Predictor from Patterns with Heuristic Origins.

satisfaction, customer See **customer satisfaction.**

satisfier A quality **characteristic**. Any feature (property or attribute) of the product, material, **process,** or service that is required to achieve **fitness for use**. These characteristics exist in several categories, including:

1. *Technological* (e.g., hardness, acidity)
2. *Psychological* (e.g., beauty, status)
3. *Time-oriented* (e.g., **reliability**, maintainability)
4. *Contractual* (e.g., guarantee provisions)
5. *Ethical* (e.g., service shop honesty, courtesy of salespeople)

scatter diagram   A graph used to analyze the relationship between two variables. Two sets of data are plotted, with the Y axis representing the variable predicted (**dependent variable**) and the X axis representing the variable making the prediction (**independent variable**). The scatter diagram shows the nature of possible relationships between the two variables. To determine if a relationship exists, the person performing the evaluation must know about the variables because an apparent relationship between two variables does not prove a relationship exists and the data are frequently analyzed using statistical tools. See Figure 41. The scatter diagram is one of the **seven basic tools of quality**.

schedule (as related to cost and quality)   See **cost/schedule/quality relationship**.

SDCA cycle   Standardize-do-check-act cycle. Similar to the **plan-do-check-act cycle**, except that the *plan* element is replaced with a **standardize** element.

1. *Standardize.* A **standard operating procedure (SOP)** is devel-

Figure 41. Scatter diagram.

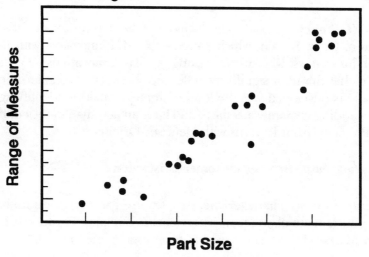

Part Size

oped, usually by a **natural work group** or by a **cross-functional team**, after one or more solutions are identified as effective in resolving a **process** problem or to reduce variability.

2. *Do*. Implement the standard operating procedure (SOP), on a pilot basis if possible.

3. *Check*. Check the effectiveness of the SOP: Is it being followed and is it clear and easy to understand? Confirm and document the effects of the action taken. This is usually accomplished through process **control chart** data and through before and after studies.

4. *Act*. Return to the *standardize* phase and make adjustments to the SOP if necessary. If the SOP is all right, implement it across all applicable areas.

See also **daily management**.

selection, employee   See **employee selection and training**.

self-managed and self-directed teams   A group of people empowered to manage their own work functions. The group is typically composed of all the individuals who perform work making up a defined **business process**.

sequential convergence   See **convergence, sequential**.

serpentine cells   A popular layout for **cellular manufacturing** operations that deploy operators inside U-shaped work cells that are connected end-to-end in a serpentine manner. See also **U-shaped cells**.

setup time reduction   An important part of reducing manufacturing **lot sizes** in order to reduce **cycle times** and **work-in-process** inventory. Setup time reductions were made popular as part of the **just-in-time manufacturing** movement in the late 1970s and early 1980s. One of the most famous practitioners in this area is Shigeo Shingo, who developed a technique called Single Minute Exchange of Dies (SMED). Reduced setup times result in smaller economic order quantities (EOQs), and thereby allow fewer parts to be manufactured in a given **lot**. There are several approaches to setup time reduction, such as dedicated setups, quick-change devices, and fixed-position mechanisms to reduce or eliminate adjustments.

seven basic tools of quality   The fundamental tools that organizations use to help understand their **processes**, which leads to their improvement. These tools are:

1. **Cause-and-effect diagrams**
2. **Check sheets**
3. **Control charts**
4. **Flow charts**
5. **Histograms**
6. **Pareto charts**
7. **Scatter diagrams**

These tools are described in more detail in separate entries within this text.

seven quality control tools   See **seven basic tools of quality**.

shape (distributional)   The visual appearance of measurements plotted on a **histogram**. Distributional shape is generally described by measures or indices of symmetry and peakedness. Specific shapes or **distributions** are described by name in other entries within this text (i.e., bell-shaped, plateau, double-peaked, and truncated). See also **skewness** and **kurtosis**, two shape **parameters**.

shareholder   Owner of a company's stock.

shareholders vs. stakeholders   Shareholders are individuals who maintain financial ownership positions in a company; partners or stockholders. They are a subset of stakeholders. Shareholders typically have a financial interest in the company, but little or no interest or involvement in day-to-day operations. Stakeholders are all of those individuals and organizations who have a significant interest in the business, not merely in the financial returns of the business. There are several categories of stakeholders, including:

1. *Government.* Who is interested in company compliance to all regulations and laws concerning the environment, employee safety, tax reporting and collection, securities regulations, and related areas such as transportation.

2. *Shareholders.* Who are interested in the return on monies invested in company stock.
3. *Executive management.* Who are interested in progress toward strategic **goals** and **objectives**, and short-term business performance, which is likely to have a direct impact on their personal financial stability and career growth.
4. *Customers.* Who are interested primarily in product or service **quality** and value. This includes product or service features, price, financing terms, and availability.
5. *Employees.* Who are interested in their own compensation, job security, personal safety, career growth, and satisfaction in their work.
6. *Suppliers.* Who are interested in a stable and growing demand (market) for their products and services, and profitability within their product lines.
7. *Community.* Who is interested in good stewardship and contribution by the company. The community appreciates the contribution of companies to the local tax base and social contributions (participation in fund-raisers, etc.). The community also wants companies to be good stewards of the local environment and resource base.

Shewhart, Walter A.   The man who created the **control chart**, who is also known as the father of **statistical quality control**. Shewhart, ASQC's first honorary member, described the basic principles of SQC in his book *Economic Control of the Quality of Manufactured Products* (New York: Van Nostrand, 1931).

Shewhart control charts   **Control charts** (X-bar, median, individuals, R, R_M, s-, np-, p-, c-, and u-charts) named for the late Dr. Walter **Shewhart**, who described the basic principles of control chart theory in his book *Economic Control of the Quality of Manufactured Products* (New York: Van Nostrand) in 1931. See also **average and range chart, s-chart, np-chart, p-chart, c-chart, R_M chart, u-chart**, and **X chart**.

Shewhart/Deming cycle   An improvement methodology attributed to **Shewhart** and **Deming** by Svenson et al. in *The Quality Roadmap* (New York: AMACOM, 1994). The methodology includes four phases:

1. *Assessment.* Data gathering and analysis to identify baseline performance and opportunities for improvement.

2. *Design and testing.* Producing a validated improvement that is ready to be deployed, using standard design and testing methodologies.
3. *Deployment.* The implementation of the improvement across the spectrum of possible applications is developed.
4. *Integration.* Integration of the improved **processes** with other processes throughout the organization.

Shingo Prize The Shingo Prize for Excellence in Manufacturing, conferred in order to promote world-class manufacturing and to recognize companies that excel in productivity and **process** improvement. Established by the late Dr. Shigeo Shingo, the prize is sponsored and managed by the Utah State University Partner's Program. The major categories of evaluation in consideration of the Shingo Prize are:

1. Total **quality** and productivity management culture and infrastructure. (See **company culture**.)
2. Manufacturing strategy, process, and systems.
3. Measured quality and productivity.
4. **Customer satisfaction**.

short-term profit See **profit, short-term**.

sigma The **standard deviation** of a **population**.

simultaneous convergence See **convergence, simultaneous**.

six sigma A term coined by Motorola to emphasize the continuous reduction of process variation. For a **normal distribution**, the probability that a value falls within $\pm\ 6\sigma$ of the mean (μ) is 99.99966%. If $\pm\ 6\sigma$ falls inside the **specification limits**, then there are only 3.4 **defects** per million parts produced from the designated **process**.

six-sigma quality program A program developed by Motorola to emphasize process variation reduction and **defects**. This program contains these key ingredients:

1. A superordinate **goal** of total **customer satisfaction**
2. Common, uniform **quality** metrics for all business areas

3. Identical improvement rate goals for all business areas
4. Goal-directed incentives for both management and employees
5. Coordinated training in why and how to achieve the goal

The program is organized in this sequence:

1. Identify the product or service to be provided.
2. Identify the **customer(s)** of the product or service.
3. Identify and communicate the need to provide a product or service that satisfies the customer. See also **communication**.
4. Define the processes performed to satisfy the customer.
5. Make the process mistake-proof and eliminate all wasted effort.
6. Ensure **continuous improvement** through process **control**.

skewed distribution   A **distribution** of data that, represented on a **histogram**, is manifested in a peak that is off-center from the midpoint of the range and tapers off much more sharply on one side of the peak than the other side. See Figure 42. See also **skewness**.

skewness   A descriptor of **shape** that indicates the degree to which a **distribution** is nonsymmetrical. Also called the third moment, or γ_3 (**population**) and g_3 (**sample**). See also **kurtosis** and **skewed distribution**.

SMED   An acronym referring to *single-minute exchange of dies,* a setup reduction technique developed by Dr. Shigeo Shingo.

SOP   See **standard operating procedure.**

span of control   The scope of responsibility over which an employee or organizational unit has direct control.

SPC   See **statistical process control**.

special causes   Specific and unusual external circumstances that result in unpredictable process variation. They are relatively few in number. Special causes are also called *assignable causes.* See also **common causes** and **process control.**

Figure 42. Skewed distributions.

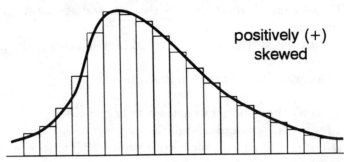

positively (+)
skewed

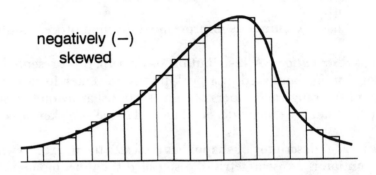

negatively (−)
skewed

specification limits   Thresholds that define acceptable ranges of the product or service **characteristics** or attributes for identifying **conformance**. In the manufacturing environment, this is often synonymous with blueprint **tolerance**. They should always reflect engineering-defined, and ultimately **customer**-defined, requirements for a **process** or product variable.

specifications   Identified requirements to which a designated service or product must conform. See also **conformance**.

spider chart   A chart used to depict and communicate **process** performance against that of a **benchmarked** company along multiple process attributes. The performance of the benchmarked company on each attribute is defined as a point on the perimeter of a polygon. A scale emanates from the center of the polygon to each point. The current performance of the company is plotted along each scale, and the points between baseline measurements are then connected, showing the performance of the company against the company benchmarked. Also called **radar chart**. See Figure 43.

sponsors Management leaders who are responsible for chartering process improvement **teams**, acting as advocates for those teams, assisting the teams in obtaining needed resources, assisting the teams by clearing roadblocks, and providing rewards and recognition to successful teams. It is not recommended that the sponsor be a member of the team. See **chartering a team**. See also **reward and recognition system**.

Figure 43. **Spider chart/radar chart.**

Customer
Satisfaction

60

Leadership

On-Time
Delivery

40

20

Inventory
Accuracy

Supplier
Quality
Assurance

Human Resource
Utilization

The top company performance in that category

Average performance of top companies in that category

Status of your company's performance

sponsor's role   The responsibilities of the **sponsor**:

1. Charge the **team** with a clear mission of what is to be accomplished.
2. Tell the **team members** why the mission is important to the operation of the business.
3. Select the initial team members and in many cases the team **leader**.
4. Work with the team leader to clarify the mission.
5. Work with the team to answer questions, help get past roadblocks, etc.
6. Provide resources to the team as necessary.
7. Help to remove organizational obstacles and barriers to team success.

SQA   See **supplier quality assurance**.

SQC   See **statistical quality control**. See also **Shewhart, Walter A.**

SQI   See **supplier quality improvement**.

stability   A measure of the dependability or consistency of a **process** over time. A process is stable if it is in control, as depicted on a process **control chart**. See also **out-of-control process**.

stages of change   As described by Svenson et al. in *The Quality Roadmap* (New York: AMACOM, 1994), there are four stages of **change** in typical TQM implementations:

Stage 1, getting started. Management begins to map the existing enterprise and gather data about **process** performance.

Stage 2, targeted improvement. Initial forays are made by way of pilot improvement projects.

Stage 3, extension to all processes. Improvements are spread across all potential applications within the company.

Stage 4, continuous improvement. Continuous process improvement becomes a way of life at the company. (See **continuous improvement**.)

stakeholders   All those inside and outside the company who have a significant interest in company performance. See **shareholders vs. stakeholders**.

standard deviation   A measure of **variability** that describes the spread of scores in a data set around the **mean**. Technically, the population standard deviation can be defined as the square root of the arithmetic average of the squares of all **deviations** from the mean in any **frequency distribution**. σ = population standard deviation; s = sample standard deviation.

standard deviation chart   See **s-chart**.

standard operating procedure (SOP)   A written document that describes the methods and procedures a worker uses to run an operation. Manufacturing SOPs typically include descriptions of the process along with the procedures that outline the following: power-up, setup, shutdown, operation, process control, adjustment, documentation, housekeeping, routine maintenance, simple troubleshooting, and diagnosis. Simple diagrams, charts, **check sheets**, flow diagrams, and visual aids may be a part of the SOP. *Note:* There are also SOPs for nonmanufacturing processes (e.g., an SOP for filing a medical claim) that do not outline power-up, maintenance, etc.

standardization   Usually means implementing a **standard operating procedure**; could also mean converting a **distribution** to a standardized **normal distribution (Z scores)**.

standardize-do-check-act cycle   See **SDCA cycle**.

standardized control charts   **Control charts** on which the observed values are translated into standardized values that represent the number of standard errors between the observed value and the **process** average.

statistical methods   Methods used to describe data and to identify levels of variation and their causes. Statistical methods may be divided into basic and advanced statistical techniques. Basic statistical methods include the graphic representation of data, basic **descriptive statistics, control chart** theory, process **control** and capability procedures for variables and **attribute data**, and underlying distributional analysis. Advanced statistical methods encompass statistical inferences, significance tests, and design and analysis of experiments.

Beyond the techniques and methods listed above, the fields of measurement, **reliability, supplier quality assurance**, procurement, testing, and others have their own applications and tools for collecting, analyzing, and interpreting statistical data in support of decision making in day-to-day business operations. See also **data collection** and **seven basic tools of quality**.

statistical process control (SPC)   The application of statistical methods to identify and reduce process variation. Typical SPC applications use SPC charts to track **process** performance in light of **control limits**. The use of these charts allows operators to monitor the performance of their processes in order to detect changes (out-of-control conditions) that may lead to unacceptable conditions or failure to capture improved conditions if left unchecked or process improvements that should be standardized. SPC charts are also used to determine when to make adjustments in order to continually reduce process **variability** toward **nominal values**. See also **out-of-control** process and **detection vs. prevention**.

statistical quality control (SQC)   A discipline that involves applying basic and advanced statistical methods and tools to **process**-related data in order to identify the critical **process variables** or **root causes** and to systematically reduce variation or eliminate problems. The **objective** of SQC is to ensure that all **customer needs** are satisfied through stable, constantly improving processes in the absence of **defects**. The basic tools of SQC are listed under **seven basic tools of quality**. These tools, as well as advanced methods, are explained in more detail in other portions of this text.

statistics, descriptive   See **descriptive statistics**.

steering committee   See discussion under **planning phase (phase II)**.

stock, buffer   See **buffer inventory/stock**.

strategic alliances   Alliances between manufacturers and their key suppliers that provide leverage in gaining access to foreign markets and offer the advantage to those suppliers of local labor content in the end item manufactured. See also **risk sharing**.

strategic goals   See **goals, strategic**.

strategic intent   A broadly based goal required to meet a competitive threat or achieve company goals. These intents result from long-term strategic analyses and plans. For example, "Achieve perferred supplier status with all critical customers" might constitute a strategic intent.

strategic objective   A short-term, specific outcome required to achieve a **strategic intent**. Usually, multiple strategic objectives must be achieved to meet a given linked intent. Further, any given set of strategic objectives must be collectively exhaustive and additive, as related to the strategic intent to which they are linked. That is, if all strategic objectives are met, it must be implicitly correct that the intent will be met.

Strategic objectives of limited scope and term, with metrics and time-based milestones, are called *focal points*. See also **focal point chart**.

strategic plan   A fundamental element of **policy deployment**, the strategic plan describes in broad terms the strategic emphases or areas of focus by which the organization intends to achieve:

1. Continuously improving levels of **customer satisfaction**
2. Continuously improving competitive position and profitability

The strategic plan typically encompasses a three- to five-year period and in TQM environments is developed in the **planning phase (phase II)** of the TQM implementation. It provides several highest-level long-term milestones against which company performance and enterprise-level progress may be monitored.

strategic product-market analysis   An analysis that provides the basis for strategic and operating planning activity. The specific structure of the analysis varies from company to company, but the content generally includes:

1. *Current practices and **processes**.* An assessment of the status of key **critical process characteristics** as they currently exist, a forecast of needs and demands of the current **customer** base compared to anticipated future demands, and a technical **benchmarking** comparison to current and potential competitors. (See also **competitor influences**.)
2. *Internal and external forces analysis.* An analysis of all significant internal and external forces affecting the products and services of the company, with associated forecasts.
3. *Growth/penetration assessment.* An assessment of the potential for growth and penetration of new markets for core competencies, products, and services.

The strategic product-market analysis should be performed late in the **preparation phase (phase I)** or early in the **planning phase (phase II)** of the TQM implementation, before the strategic planning activity.

subgroup   A set of units or observations obtained by subdividing a larger group of units or observations.

suggestion systems   A means by which employees (and stakeholders) can offer their ideas. The purpose of an employee suggestion system is to provide an opportunity for individuals with the company to contribute to achievement of the company's strategic goals. (See **goals, strategic**.) It resides in the **employee involvement** element of the TQM model, is focused on the employee, and is generally administered by first-line supervision.

The suggestion program within the TQM model is unlike stand-alone suggestion programs in that it is focused on specific topics for improvement that have been identified as a part of **policy deployment**, and it operates within the department's **span of control**, making it easier to administer. In addition, TQM-based suggestion programs support suggester-led evaluations of the suggestion, and orient the suggestions toward specific results identified as ways to improve overall **processes** and systems. Those offering suggestions play an active role in implementing their suggestions.

supplier   A person, group, or organization (internal or external) from whom goods or services are obtained.

supplier cost of quality accounting systems   One component of the **supplier quality assurance** system model, which provides the detailed data required to analyze the total cost (as opposed to price) of products from suppliers. See also **cost of quality** and **total cost concept in purchasing.**

supplier quality assurance   Confidence that a supplier's product or service will meet its **customers'** requirements. A data-based relationship is developed between the **customer** and the **supplier** that ensures that products and services delivered satisfy (and eventually exceed) **customer needs**. A component of the **total quality assurance** part of the TQM model, which includes supplier selection and qualification, **cost of quality**, and specification approval and review system. See Figure 44. See also **customer satisfaction.**

supplier quality improvement   As an element of TQM, supplier quality improvement programs should involve three major elements:

Figure 44. A suggested model for a supplier quality assurance system.

1. Including key suppliers in the **design review** process
2. Requiring suppliers to adopt a management philosophy of **continuous improvement**, founded in TQM principles
3. Inviting key suppliers who have adopted a TQM approach to become **risk-sharing** partners in new development projects where they are significant **stakeholders**

supplier selection and qualification　　One component of the **supplier quality assurance** system model, dedicated to the analysis and selection of **supplier, faciliation** and improvement responsibilities, and purchased product/component analysis. Among the elements contained in the supplier selection and qualification system are:

1. The ongoing supplier review system (including on-site supplier support and assistance, and on-site SQA performance evaluations)
2. The internal supplier assessment and qualification system (including an assessment of price and delivery performance, as well as an evaluation of the supplier's product **quality** as it relates to downstream process variation)

support processes　　**Processes** that support the primary value-adding processes of the company. These processes include human resources, accounting, and information technology management. See also **value-added analysis**.

survey-feedback process　　The process developed and used by a company to continuously receive feedback from its **customers** and **suppliers** regarding its performance. (See also **feedback, customer**.) This process is an important source of information in the first two phases of a TQM implementation and is also critical to the **continuous improvement** effort contained in the last phase of TQM implementation. The process is designed differently in virtually every company, but the most important aspects are the same: the process must yield accurate, usable, and timely information about the perceptions of customers and suppliers concerning the **quality** of the company.

synchronous production　　An approach used in **just-in-time manufacturing** that synchronizes the rate of production from end item delivery all the way back through supplier production to **customer** demand. In other words, products are built at the same rate at which they are sold. See also **uniform work loading**.

T

tactical metrics   Measurements that are tracked to maintain critical tactical items—those things that must be maintained while working on strategic objectives and focal point items. For example, if reducing delivery time is a strategic objective, a critical tactical objective may be to maintain inventory. Hence, inventory would be a critical item and *days inventory* may be a critical tactical metric.

Taguchi, Genichi   A Japanese **quality** leader whose work in the 1950s popularized the idea that poor quality results in a loss to society. He is also famous for his work with orthogonal arrays and fractional factorial experiments.

Taguchi loss function   A parabolic representation that estimates the **quality** loss, expressed monetarily, that results when quality **characteristics** (**satisfiers**) deviate from **target values**.
   The cost of this **deviation** increases quadratically as the characteristic moves farther from the target value. This model is named for Genichi **Taguchi**, who won the **Deming Prize** in 1961 for his paper based on this topic. See Figure 45.

Figure 45. **Taguchi loss function.**

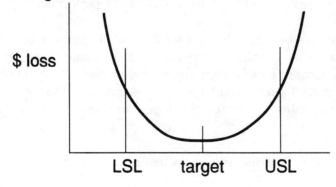

Taguchi quality loss function   See **Taguchi loss function**.

tally sheet   See **check sheet**.

target population   See **population**.

target value   The value given to a **process** owner to "hit" in ongoing production and **control**. If possible, the target will be equivalent to the **nominal value** for the product or process **characteristic**. Where nominal is closer to one **specification** than another, the target may be different from the nominal value to avoid the production of nonconforming units.

team, chartering a   See **chartering a team**.

team, cross-functional   See **cross-functional team**.

team, steering   See **steering teams**.

team member's role   The responsibilities of the team member:

1. Help ensure balanced participation among all team members.
2. Attend team meetings.
3. Identify opportunities for improvement of team interaction.
4. Carry out action items (assigned tasks/responsibilities).
5. Clarify individual understanding of the team mission.
6. Follow the team's ground rules.
7. Learn the structured process the team uses.
8. Recognize and communicate the need for training.
9. Ensure closure on items.
10. Share responsibility for team members' performance.

teams   Groups of people formed for the specific purpose of improving **quality** or solving problems. The teams may be **natural work groups** or cross-functional in membership, depending on the nature of the subject matter they are formed to address. See **sponsors**; **facilitator**; **leader, team**; and **team member's role**. See also **cross-functional team** and **problem solving**.

technique error   See **operator-controllable error**.

technology migration paths   The most likely paths of migration of a new technology through an organization. These paths are predominantly downstream through the internal supplier-customer structure, but may vary depending on several other factors, as described in *Manufacturing 2000* (New York, AMACOM, 1994.)

telecommuting   Performing work from a remote location via telecommunications and/or computer equipment. Typically, this involves the use of personal computers, telephone lines, and a telecommunications device (modem) on each end that translates the computer's language into transmittable signals and back again.

TEQA   See **European Quality Award**.

testing   See **destructive testing** and **nondestructive testing**.

Theory X   A theory of behavior that suggests and acts on the belief that people are basically lazy, find work repulsive, and prefer to be directed in their work activities.

Theory Y   A theory of behavior that hypothesizes and acts on the belief that people are self-motivated, enjoy work, and prefer to think for themselves, remaining at least semi-autonomous in their work activity.

Theory Z   A theory of behavior that emphasizes fair treatment of **customers**, production of **quality** products, and other traits/values that would generally be regarded favorably.

third-party registration   Certification by an independent registrar as compliant with one or more **ISO 9000** standards. See **registration, ISO 9000**.

throughput time   See **cycle time**.

tolerance   The maximum acceptable **deviation** from specified **target value**. The amount of tolerance is listed in the **specification** or on the blueprint for a quality **characteristic**.

tool wear   A condition under which the **variability** of the **process** at any one point in time will be less than the **distribution** over the life of the tool.

tooling reliability   The probability that a given tool will produce parts within **control limits**. Poor tooling **reliability** is usually symptomatic of a more fundamental problem. It is important to look for the more fundamental problem (e.g., machine vibration) and solve it in order to maintain long-term process **control**.

total cost concept in purchasing   The concept that the true cost of a purchased item is the cost associated with procurement and use of the item. See also **supplier cost of quality accounting systems**.

total predictive maintenance   See **predictive maintenance**.

total productive maintenance (TPM)   A representation of overall equipment effectiveness using mathematical models of losses (associated with the manufacturing **process**) due to equipment **failure**, setup and adjustment, idling and minor stoppage, reduced speed, process **defects**, and reduced yield.

total quality assurance (TQA)   One of three interlocking technologies supporting the management subsystems of TQM. **Customer** driven, it supports **daily management**, the **PDCA management discipline**, and **policy deployment**. It focuses on **prevention** rather than **detection** through design and process **control**, and may be subdivided into the components of **supplier quality assurance**, **statistical quality control**, and **customer quality assurance**. See also **detection vs. prevention**, **quality improvement strategy**, and **problem solving**.

total quality control (TQC)   An approach to **quality** that focuses on assuring the quality of all the inputs to a system, including materials, information, labor, and equipment. TQC (also referred to as SQC) is often regarded as the subset of TQM from which the **plan-do-check-act cycle** approach emerged.

total quality management (TQM)   A term initially coined by the Naval Air Systems Command to describe its Japanese-style management approach to **quality** improvement. Since then, the term *TQM* has taken on many meanings. Simply stated, TQM is a system by which continuous improvement of all value-adding processes performed by the organization may be achieved. The **customer** determines if value has been added based on his or her satisfaction. (See **customer satisfaction** and **value-added analysis**.)

TQM is predicated on the participation of each organization member in improving products, **processes**, services, and the **company culture**. The methods used in TQM have been developed from earlier work by quality leaders such as W. Edwards **Deming**, Armand V. **Feigenbaum**, Kaoru **Ishikawa**, and Joseph M. **Juran**.

total quality management system (TQMS)   The consistent, structured application of management commitment, **leadership**, **customer** focus, total participation, and systematic analysis to an organization's processes in order to achieve **customer satisfaction**.

TPM   See **total productive maintenance**.

TQA   See **total quality assurance**.

TQC   See **total quality control**.

TQM   See **total quality management**.

TQMS   See **total quality management system**.

tracking, attributes   See **attributes tracking**.

training   An educational tool used to develop and improve skills, which must be present for quality improvement. Training for TQM practitioners is tailored to the needs of the individual, based on:

1. *Roles*. Management roles are very different from floor-level process improvement **team member roles**, so their skills requirements differ.
2. *Timing*. It is best to administer training when there is a clear and present need for the training.
3. *Cost/availability*. Both help determine the feasibility of training initiatives.

Among the most frequently included training for TQM practitioners are the following topics:

- The **seven basic tools of quality**
- **Statistical process control**

- **Benchmarking**
- **Quality function deployment**
- **Problem-solving strategy**
- **Quality improvement strategy**
- Industrial statistics
- **Design of experiments**
- Team effectiveness
  Basic TQM awareness
- New roles for TQM leaders (managers and supervisors)

See also **education and training (for total quality)** and **employee selection and training**.

trend   A series of six or more measurements that represent progressively increasing or progressively decreasing values. Nonrandom behavior. A trend indicates an out-of-control condition and the presence of an assignable (special) cause. See also **special cause**, **process control**, and **out-of-control process**.

trivial many   In the context of **Pareto analysis**, a reference to the majority (roughly 80%) of occurrences in a **population** of occurrences representing 20% of the value of the population. (**Juran** referred to this group as the *important many* since they often, in fact, hold value.) See also **vital few**.

true value   The theoretically correct and actual value of the **characteristic** being measured.

truncated distribution   On a **histogram**, an asymmetrical **shape** with the peak at or near one end of the data range, and with the data range falling off abruptly at one end, while the other end of the **distribution** tapers off gently. Truncated distributions often result from abnormal effects on the data gathered, such as screening the data by employing 100% **inspection** and reworking the **defective** parts before their values are counted in the distribution. See Figure 46.

tweaking   Action taken to compensate for **common causes** of variation, which often has the effect of increasing rather than decreasing the variation.

Figure 46. **Truncated distribution.**

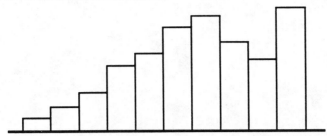

Type I error An incorrect decision to reject a **hypothesis** when it is really true. See also **alpha**.

Type II error An incorrect decision to accept a **hypothesis** that is really false. See also **beta**.

U

u-chart   A **control chart** based on the normal approximation to the **Poisson distribution**, which depicts the **defect** count per **inspection** unit.

U-shaped cells   In **cellular manufacturing**, work centers configured in horizontal U shapes, with operators occupying positions within the U. This configuration allows operators to more easily move between positions, adjusting the number of operators in a cell based on the work load present at a given time. The U-shaped layout is illustrated under **cellular manufacturing**.

UCL   See **upper control limit**.

unexplained variation   See **experimental error**.

uniform work loading   Matching the **cycle times** of individual operations within the production routing, so that production occurs as if to a common drum beat. This is synonymous with **synchronous production**, except that synchronous production goes even further, matching production to end item delivery rates.

universe   See **population**.

upper control limit (UCL)   The upper boundary, drawn as a horizontal dashed line on a **control chart**, indicating the value below which sample (statistical) values are expected to fall due to **common causes** of variation. A full and proper assessment of control requires consideration of process performance with respect to the **lower control limit** and the laws of probability in addition to the upper control limit. See **control limit** and **in-control process**.

upper limit (UL) A term used by different practitioners to refer (ambiguously) to **upper specification limit**, **upper process limit**, or **upper control limit**.

upper process limit The threshold above which exactly .135% of the measures, scores, values, or observations fall.

upper specification limit (USL) The threshold above which the **characteristic** being measured is considered to be **defective**, because it no longer conforms to **specifications**. See also **conformance**.

USL See **upper specification limit**.

V

value The result of the benefit one receives from a product or service relative to what was expended to receive or acquire it. Generally value is the ratio of benefit to cost, and more specifically, value is the ratio of quality to cost or quality to price. Cost in this case is not just the purchase price, but refers to all of the costs the customer incurs for the privilege of using a product or service. To increase value, one can increase the benefit to the customer through increased **quality** or by more effectively meeting expectations. Value is also increased by reducing the price or cost to the customer. Those organizations able to both increase quality and decrease (total) cost to the customer benefit greatly.

value, adding See **adding value**.

value, nominal See **nominal value**.

value, target See **target value**.

value, true See **true value**.

value-added analysis An analysis performed on a **process** to determine which elements of that process add **value**, and how much throughput time and **work-in-process** results from that non-value-added activity.

value-adding process An activity that transforms an input into a more valuable output to be used by a **customer**. The customer may be part of the organization performing the activity or may be an external customer. See also **adding value**.

value analysis/value engineering A structured technique developed by Value Analysis, Incorporated, in 1963, which formally analyzes **processes** and designs for the sole purpose of reducing cost and **waste** in those processes and designs.

values, organizational   See **organizational values**.

variability   Changes in data, a **characteristic**, or a function caused by one of four factors: assignable or **special causes**, **common causes**, **tweaking**, or seasonal/long-term **trends**.

variable, dependent or response   See **dependent variable**.

variable, process   See **critical process characteristics**.

variables data   Quantifiable, measurable, **continuous data**. Variable-based **control charts** include X-bar, R, median, X, s, and moving range (R_M).

variance   A measure of **dispersion** that is equal to the squared **standard deviation**.

variance, analysis of   See **analysis of variance**.

variation, environment's role   See **environment and variation**.

variation, unexplained   See **experimental error**.

verification, design   See **design verification**.

virtual reality   A particularly vivid form of computer simulation that generates the feeling that a person is physically at some remote location through the use of devices that provide multiple sensory inputs (visual, audio, tactile, etc.).

vision, development of   The development of the **vision** and **vision statement**. This process should be performed by the company's top-level management and/or owner(s). Visions result from people answering tough questions about exactly what business(es) they desire in five to ten years, why, and generally how they plan to get there. They must envision their size, location, and operating methods. They must base all of these elements on an even more fundamental and important question: What is the purpose of this company?

vision (company/corporate)   The company's purpose for existence, the standards and behaviors or guiding principles that the company exhibits, and the overall strategy the company intends to use to achieve its objectives. See **vision statement** and **vision, development of.**

vision statement   A fundamental element of **policy deployment.** The **vision** statement describes the underlying premises on which the company is based, and more importantly, describes in a compelling way where the company is going to be at some future point. It is critical to gaining shared **goals** and **objectives** within the company, and to generating enthusiastic participation in broad, sweeping **changes** such as TQM implementation. Impactful vision statements create employee commitment, not just compliance.

vital few   A term emerging from the **Pareto analysis,** which refers to the minority (roughly 20%) of any **population,** which represents the majority (roughly 80%) of the value of the population. See also **trivial many.**

voice of the customer   See **customer mapping process.**

W

WANs   See **wide area networks**.

waste   Any expenditure of resources (including time) that does not add value in terms of a **customer**-satisfying quality **characteristic** (**satisfier**). See also **value-added analysis**.

Weibull distribution/plots   Graphic representations of the Weibull family of **distributions**, described by three **parameters**: shape, scale, and location. The **shape** parameter (ß) establishes the pattern of the curve; the scale **parameter** (α) is related to the peakedness of the curve; and the location parameter (γ) is the origin, or starting point, and has a default value of zero. See Figure 47.

Figure 47. **Weibull distribution.**

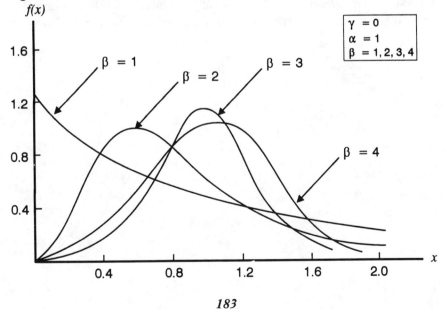

wide area networks (WANs)   Computer networks similar in function to today's local area networks (LANs), where multiple users are supported by servers on a host computer, except that the scale is much greater. WANs developed over the next several years will connect multiple LANs and other remote facilities with voice, data, and image transmission.

WIP   See **work-in-process**.

work content study   A detailed study of the specific tasks performed in a designated **process**. A work content study identifies all tasks as value-adding or non-value-adding, identifies the time and resources required for each task, and identifies the skills required for the performance of each task. It is typically performed as part of a throughput time-reduction effort in **just-in-time manufacturing** programs, but is also very effective in non-manufacturing businesses. See also **value-added analysis**.

work-in-process (WIP)   Any inventory against which direct labor has been applied and has not yet been completed. One of three categories of inventory: raw material, work-in-process, and finished goods.

world class   As good as, or better than, anyone else in the business in which a company is involved. "Good" in this context means "able to identify and satisfy the needs of the **customer**."

world-class manufacturing   As good as, or better than, any other company offering the same types of manufactured products. See also **world class**.

$\widetilde{X}, R$ *chart*   See **median and range chart**.

X, R_M *chart*   Individuals and moving range chart. See **X chart** and **R_M chart**.

X-bar and R ($\overline{X}, R$) chart   See **average and range chart**.

X-bar and standard deviation ($\overline{X}, s$) charts   Variables **control charts** containing the data that would normally appear on an **X-bar chart** and a **standard deviation** chart. These charts are used most often for high-volume processes and when large **sample sizes** are involved ($n \geq 8$ per **subgroup**).

X-bar charts   Sample average **control charts**.

X chart   Individuals chart. Variables **control chart** that plots individual measurements (vs. **subgroups**) for each time period.

yield   See **recovery**.

Z

Z score   The number of **standard deviations** separating a given value from the **mean** of a **distribution**. A standardized value used to transform a **continuous data** set into a standard normal distribution (a **normal distribution** with a mean of zero and a standard deviation of one).

zero defects   A **quality** philosophy that advocates a focus on error-free **process** performance, resulting in **defect**-free products and/or services.